CW01304277

Lean

What You Need to Know About Lean Six Sigma, Agile Project Management, Scrum and Kanban

© Copyright 2020

All Rights Reserved. No part of this book may be reproduced in any form without permission in writing from the author. Reviewers may quote brief passages in reviews.

Disclaimer: No part of this publication may be reproduced or transmitted in any form or by any means, mechanical or electronic, including photocopying or recording, or by any information storage and retrieval system, or transmitted by email without permission in writing from the publisher.

While all attempts have been made to verify the information provided in this publication, neither the author nor the publisher assumes any responsibility for errors, omissions or contrary interpretations of the subject matter herein.

This book is for entertainment purposes only. The views expressed are those of the author alone, and should not be taken as expert instruction or commands. The reader is responsible for his or her own actions.

Adherence to all applicable laws and regulations, including international, federal, state and local laws governing professional licensing, business practices, advertising and all other aspects of doing business in the US, Canada, UK or any other jurisdiction is the sole responsibility of the purchaser or reader.

Neither the author nor the publisher assumes any responsibility or liability whatsoever on the behalf of the purchaser or reader of these materials. Any perceived slight of any individual or organization is purely unintentional.

Contents

PART 1: LEAN METHODOLOGY 0
INTRODUCTION 1
PART ONE: PROJECT MANAGEMENT BASICS 3
CHAPTER ONE: PROJECT MANAGEMENT METHODOLOGIES 4
    WHAT IS PROJECT MANAGEMENT? 4
    PROJECT MANAGEMENT METHODOLOGIES 5
        Agile 6
        Scrum 8
        Events 8
        Scrum Artifacts 9
        Kanban 9
        Lean 11
        Waterfall 13
        Six Sigma 13
        PMI/PMBOK 15
CHAPTER TWO: THE PROJECT MANAGER ROLE 17
    WHO IS A PROJECT MANAGER? 17
    ROLES AND RESPONSIBILITIES OF PROJECT MANAGERS 18

  Resource and Activity Planning 18

  Motivating and Organizing the Team 18

  Time Management 19

  Estimating Cost and Developing the Budget 19

  Ensuring Customer Satisfaction 19

  Identifying and Managing Project Risk 19

  Monitoring Progress 20

  Managing Necessary Documentation and Reports 20

 Do you need a Project Manager? 20

CHAPTER THREE: CHOOSING THE RIGHT METHODOLOGY 22

 Benefits of Choosing an Organizational PM Method 22

 Choosing the Right Method 23

 Software 24

  Gantt Charts 25

  Kanban Boards 25

  Calendars 25

  Mobile Accessibility 25

  Cross-Project Summary Views 26

PART TWO: LEAN PROJECT MANAGEMENT 27

CHAPTER FOUR: WHAT IS LEAN? 28

 Lean Management for Production and Services 29

 Lean Business Principles 29

  Perfection 29

  Value Identification 30

  Value Stream Mapping 30

  Flow 30

  Pull 31

 Lean Tools 31

  Takt Time 31

Continuous Flow 31
Standardized Work 32
Kanban and Pull Systems 32
Cellular Manufacturing 32
The Why's 32
Level the Workload 33
Problem Solving 33

CHAPTER FIVE: START A LEAN PROJECT 34

INITIATION 34
PLANNING 34
EXECUTION 35
Flow 35
Inventory 35
Kaizen 36
MONITORING & CONTROL 36
CLOSING 36

CHAPTER SIX: LEAN SIX SIGMA 38

SIMILARITIES OF LEAN AND SIX SIGMA 38
WHAT IS THE DIFFERENCE BETWEEN LEAN AND SIX SIGMA? 40
LEAN SIX SIGMA PRINCIPLES 41
Addressing a Real-World Problem 41
A Team Accomplishes Analysis 42
The Analysis is Focused on a Process 42
The Analysis is Based on Data 43
Understand the Impact of the Process Sigma 44
The Solution Addresses the Real Root Cause(s) 45
BENEFITS OF LEAN SIX SIGMA 46
Organizational Benefits 46
Personal Benefits 48

INDUSTRIES AND FUNCTIONS USING LEAN SIX SIGMA 49

CHAPTER SEVEN: LEAN STARTUP 52

   PRINCIPLES OF LEAN STARTUP 53

      Validated Learning 53

      Entrepreneurs are Everywhere 53

      Controlled Use and Deployment of Resources 53

      Entrepreneurship is Management 54

      Build-Measure-Learn 54

   MODELS AND METHODOLOGIES 54

      Build-Measure-Learn 55

      Minimal Viable Product (MVP) 55

      Validated Learning 56

      Innovation Accounting 56

      Persevere or Pivot 57

      Small Batches 59

      Andon Cord 60

      Continuous Deployment 60

      Kanban 60

      The Five Whys 61

CHAPTER EIGHT: LEAN ENTERPRISE 64

   HOW TO START TO CREATE A LEAN ENTERPRISE 64

   THE DIFFICULTIES OF THE FLOW OF INFORMATION 65

   SIPOC TO STANDARDIZE THE INFORMATION FLOW 66

CHAPTER NINE: LEAN TEAMS 68

   DEVELOPING A LEAN TEAM 68

   FORMING A TEAM 68

   EMPOWERING THE TEAM 69

   LEAN TEAM HIERARCHY 70

   IMPLEMENTING A LEAN TEAM 70

- *Kaizen* 71
- *Five Whys* 71
- *PDCA* 71
- How to Build a Lean Team 71
  - *Start Small* 72
  - *Make the Team Cross-Functional* 72
  - *Never Over-Rely on Team Players* 73
  - *Train People to Be Team Smart* 73
  - *Creating a Pro-Risk Environment* 74
  - *Understanding the Needs of the Team* 75
  - *Measure to Learn and Improve the Team* 75

CHAPTER TEN: WHAT IS LEAN ANALYTICS? 77

- What Kind of Business Are You? 77
  - *Empathy* 78
  - *Stickiness* 78
  - *Virality* 78
  - *Revenue* 78
  - *Scale* 78
- How to Apply Lean Analytics 78
  - *Trigger* 79
  - *Action* 79
  - *Variable Reward* 79
  - *Investment* 80
- How to Use the Lean Analytics Canvas 80

PART THREE: AGILE PROJECT MANAGEMENT 81

CHAPTER ELEVEN: WHAT IS THE AGILE FRAMEWORK? 82

- Which Framework is Best? 83
- Scrum, Extreme Programming and Kanban 83
- The Agile Manifesto 84

AGILE PRINCIPLES 85

PLATINUM PRINCIPLES 87

    Visualize Instead of Writing 87

    Think and Act as a Team 88

    Avoiding Formality 88

CHAPTER TWELVE: START AN AGILE PROJECT 90

UNDERSTANDING AGILE PROJECT MANAGEMENT 90

    Understand the Problem 91

    Assemble the Right Team 91

    Brainstorm 91

    Build an Initial Prototype 91

    Decide the Boundaries 92

    Plan the Major Milestones Using A Roadmap 92

    Plan Sprints 92

    Check In Every Day 93

    Review the Sprint 93

    Plan the Next Sprint 93

    Completion and Release 94

CHAPTER THIRTEEN: AGILE VERSUS SCRUM VERSUS KANBAN 95

DIFFERENCES BETWEEN AGILE, KANBAN AND SCRUM 95

DIFFERENCES BETWEEN SCRUM AND KANBAN 96

    Product Owner 96

    Scrum Master 97

    Team Members 97

AGILE PROS AND CONS 97

SCRUM PROS AND CONS 98

KANBAN PROS AND CONS 98

WHICH ONE SHOULD YOU CHOOSE? 99

CHAPTER FOURTEEN: STEP-BY-STEP SCRUM 100

BASICS OF SCRUM 101
THE ROADMAP TO VALUE 102
A SIMPLE OVERVIEW 103
   Product Backlog *103*
   Teams *104*
GOVERNANCE 105
   Product Owner *105*
   Development Team *105*
   Scrum Master *106*
SCRUM FRAMEWORK 106
   Artifacts *107*
   Roles *107*
   Events *107*
FEEDBACK 108
STEPS TO FOLLOW 109
   Define the Scrum Team *109*
   Define the Sprint Length *109*
   Appoint the Scrum Master *109*
   Appoint the Product Owner *110*
   Create the Initial Backlog *110*
   Plan the Start of The First Sprint *110*
   Close the Current Sprint and Start the Next One *111*

CHAPTER FIFTEEN: CREATE A KANBAN PROJECT 112
A BRIEF HISTORY 112
WHAT IS THE KANBAN METHOD? 113
KANBAN CHANGE MANAGEMENT PRINCIPLES 113
FOUNDATIONAL PRINCIPLES 114
   Always start with what you are doing now *114*
   Pursue Evolutionary and Incremental Change *114*

- Respect Current Roles, Responsibilities, and Designations 114
- Encourage Acts of Leadership 114
- CORE PRACTICES 114
  - Visualize the Workflow 114
  - Limit or Reduce Work-in-Progress 115
  - Manage Flow 116
  - Make Policies Explicit 116
  - Feedback Loops 117
  - Improve and Evolve Collaboratively and Experimentally 117
- IMPLEMENTING KANBAN 118
  - Step One: Visualization Of Workflow 118
  - Step Two: Limit the Amount of WIP 118
  - Step Three: Switch to Explicit Policies 119
  - Step Four: Measure and Manage the Workflow 119
  - Step Five: Using Scientific Methods for Optimization 119

CONCLUSION 120

PART 2: LEAN SIX SIGMA 121

A PRACTICAL GUIDE FOR GETTING STARTED WITH LEAN SIX SIGMA ALONG WITH HOW IT CAN BE INTEGRATED WITH AGILE AND SCRUM 121

INTRODUCTION 122

CHAPTER 1. WHAT IS LEAN PROJECT MANAGEMENT? 126
- THE ORIGINS OF LEAN 129
- LEAN PRINCIPLES AND BENEFITS 131
- LEAN BENEFITS AND WASTE 136

CHAPTER 2. SIX SIGMA: TOOLS, ROLES, AND CONCEPTS 140
- THE ORIGINS OF SIX SIGMA 144
- KEY ELEMENTS AND ROLES 145
- GETTING STARTED: THE STEPS AND TOOLS 148

CHAPTER 3. LEAN + SIX SIGMA = LEAN SIX SIGMA 154
CHAPTER 4. TRAINING AND CERTIFICATIONS: WHAT DO I NEED? 159
CHAPTER 5. THE LEAN SIX SIGMA PROCESS: DMAIC VS DMADV.162
DMAIC 162
DMADV 165
DMAIC VS DMADV 169
CHAPTER 6. DEFINE: PROCESS MAPPING AND CUSTOMER VOICE 172
WHAT IS THE DEFINE PHASE? 172
PROCESS MAPPING: SIPOC 174
VOICE OF THE CUSTOMER: IDENTIFYING AND UNDERSTANDING CUSTOMERS.179
CHAPTER 7. MEASURE: PROJECT WHY'S, DATA, AND DEFECTS...182
WHAT IS THE MEASURE PHASE? 183
DATA TYPES AND DATA COLLECTION 185
IDENTIFYING PROJECT YS 186
VARIATIONS AND DEFECTS 187
CHAPTER 8. ANALYZE: FINDING POSSIBLE AND ROOT CAUSES...190
WHAT IS THE ANALYZE PHASE? 191
VALUE STREAM MAPPING: IDENTIFYING WASTE CAUSES 193
THE FIVE WHYS METHOD 194
HYPOTHESIS TESTING 196
CHAPTER 9. IMPROVE: GENERATING SOLUTIONS 199
WHAT IS THE IMPROVE PHASE? 199
STEPS TOWARD IMPROVEMENT 200
COST-BENEFIT ANALYSIS 201
SOLUTION PARAMETERS AND GENERATING POSSIBLE SOLUTIONS..................204
CHAPTER 10. CONTROL: SUSTAINING IMPROVEMENT 207
WHAT IS THE CONTROL PHASE? 208

THE CONTROL PLAN 209

CONTROL CHART 210

MISTAKE PROOFING: POKA YOKE 212

CHAPTER 11. LEAN SIX SIGMA WITH AGILE AND SCRUM 216

CHAPTER 12. MISTAKES TO AVOID IN LEAN SIX SIGMA 221

CONCLUSION 225

RESOURCES 229

Part 1: Lean Methodology

A Guide to Lean Six Sigma, Agile Project Management, Scrum and Kanban for Beginners

Introduction

You may have come across the phrase, "Life is what happens to you while you are busy making other plans." This applies to a business, too. A business should learn to change or adapt to change since things never go according to plan. The same can be said about the different teams in an organization. In this era of technology, many businesses are shifting toward artificial intelligence and automation. A machine can perform different processes. For example, if you own a company that sells cassettes, you know you cannot make sales because the world has moved on from cassettes to storing music on mobile devices. The same can be said about some processes in an organization.

Many processes in organizations become redundant over a period, and they should be removed from the organization. It is only when the business can do this that it can apply one of the new-age project management methodologies. Throughout this book, you will gather information about the basics of project management. You will learn more about what the role of a project manager is and how you should choose the right methodology for your project.

Numerous project management methodologies have been developed to improve businesses and processes. You must understand these methodologies to ensure that you know what method to choose. Having said that, you cannot expect a method that worked in one company to work in yours. Each team is different, and the same goes for your team, too. When you choose a project management methodology for your team or business, remember that you need to tweak the method so that it works well for you and your team.

This book also sheds some light on methodologies like Lean and Agile. You will gather information about lean project management and learn more about the different components of lean project management. You will gather information on how to start a lean project and also learn more about lean six sigma. The book also details the agile framework and addresses the different methodologies that come under the umbrella of the agile framework. It is only when you fully understand these concepts that you can work better with your teams.

PART ONE: Project Management Basics

Chapter One: Project Management Methodologies

What Is Project Management?

A project is often a temporary undertaking for creating a specific service, product, or obtaining the desired result. The scope and resources involved for completing a project are always defined along with the time taken for its completion. Apart from this, the dates on which the project will start and end are also identified. In this sense, the project is a temporary endeavor. A project is different from all the other routine operations taking place in an organization. It has a unique purpose and includes specific operations that are designed with the sole purpose of attaining unique goals. All the members present in a project work towards attaining a singular goal. It means that even those employees who don't usually work together are clubbed together for attaining these goals. All the members of a project team don't necessarily have to be from the same organization and, at times, are from different organizations across various geographies. Creation of software to streamline business operations, constructing a new building, working together after a natural calamity, and expanding into new markets are all examples of projects.

Given the complexity of a project, it is quintessential that they are thoroughly managed for delivering results on time while sticking to the budget forecast. Therefore, project management is the application of different skills, tools, knowledge, and techniques associated with all project-related activities for obtaining the project goals. Project management has always been a part of any organization or enterprise. However, it was only during the mid-twentieth century that it was recognized as a distinct profession. There are five processes involved in any project management, and they are initiation, planning, execution, monitoring and control, and closing.

Integration, scope, cost, time, quality, human resources, procurement, communications, stakeholder management, and risk management are all the different areas of knowledge involved in project management. Management is often concerned with all these areas. However, project management does lend a unique focus based on the goals, resources, and schedules associated with each project.

Project Management Methodologies

Project management methodology refers to the different practices, techniques, rules, and procedures used by a project manager. Examples of project management methodologies include Six Sigma, Kanban, Agile, and so on. These methodologies encompass different processes that offer guidance to project managers through different stages of a project and enable them to complete various tasks involved. They essentially help to manage and maximize the resources as well as the time available.

Selecting the right project management methodology is an important duty. Project managers understand its importance since it is essential for getting the work done effectively and efficiently. There are different types of project management methodologies, and no one size fits all solution is available. In fact, there is no such thing as the right methodology that the manager can choose—it principally means that you cannot opt for one methodology for all the different projects you undertake. Depending on the scope and requirements of the project, the management methodology you use will change. In this section, you will learn about the most popular project management methodologies.

Agile

One of the popular project management methodologies today is Agile. It is well-suited for all such projects that are incremental and iterative. It consists of processes wherein demands as well as solutions are obtained via collaborative efforts of cross-functional teams, self-organization, and the customers. Initially, it was created with the aim of software development. Agile was established to cope with the shortcomings of the Waterfall method. The processes of this were incapable of meeting the various demands of an extremely competitive and constantly changing environment of the software industry.

The values, as well as the principles of Agile project management methodology, are obtained from the Agile manifesto. Thirteen industry leaders formalized this declaration in 2001. Agile project management aimed to come up with different ways to develop software by providing a measurable and clear structure. This structure supports iterative development, recognition of changes, and provides a framework for team collaborations. There are twelve key principles, along with four fundamental values that form the basis of Agile project management methodology.

The values of this methodology are as follows:

- Emphasis is placed on interactions as well as individuals, more than on the tools and processes involved.

- Priority is given to customer collaboration instead of contract negotiation.

- Instead of comprehensive documentation, this framework enables the working of the software.

- Instead of blindly following a plan, Agile methodology fosters better responses to change.

- The principles of this management methodology are as follows:

1. Customer satisfaction is ensured via continuous and early software delivery.

2. The requirements of a project keep changing throughout the developmental process. Agile management helps accommodate all of these requirements.

3. Continuous delivery of working software.

4. It provides a basis for collaborative efforts between developers as well as the business stakeholders during the entire duration of the project.

5. It helps foster trust, motivation, and support amongst all those who are involved.

6. It increases the scope for face-to-face interactions.

7. The primary measure of progress used in this methodology is the working software.

8. It creates a basis for the consistent and continuous pace of development.

9. The simplicity it offers is unlike other methodologies.

10. Great attention to design and technical details.

11. The self-organization of teams prompts the development of designs, requirements, and architectures.

12. It provides scope for regular reviews to improve effectiveness.

The adaptiveness of Agile methodology comes in handy, especially while working on complex projects. It uses different deliverables to measure and track progress to help with project completion and product development. The six deliverables used by Agile include release plan, vision statement, product backlog, sprint backlog, increment, and product roadmap. Because of these features, the main emphasis of this methodology is flexibility, frequent improvements, collaboration, and delivering high-quality outputs.

Scrum

The five values of Scrum are based on include respect, commitment, openness, focus, and courage. The primary goal of Scrum is to help with the development, delivery, and the sustenance of complex products. All this is attained via collaboration, iterative progress, and accountability. The main factor that differentiates Scrum from Agile project management is that it functions using specific events, roles, and artifacts. These three factors will now be looked at in detail.

Team Roles

There are three team roles available in Scrum management: product owners, the development team, and the Scrum Master. The product owner, as the name suggests, represents all the stakeholders as well as potential customers. The development team comprises of different professionals who help and deliver the product, such as programmers, designers, and developers. The third category includes an organized manager who helps understand and execute how Scrum has to be followed.

Events

There are five events included in Scrum: Sprint, Sprint Planning, Daily Scrum, Sprint review, and sprint retrospective. Sprint is the term used for the iterative time boxes within which a goal has to be attained. The timeframe for every individual box is one calendar month, and it cannot exceed this timeframe. Also, the same will be consistent throughout the development process. Whenever the Scrum team gets together, usually at the beginning of the Sprint, it is known as Sprint planning. During this meeting, the team plans for the Sprint. Daily Scrum refers to fifteen minutes of the daily meeting, which will be held at the same time consistently. In this meeting, a review of the previous day's progress is discussed, along with any expectations for the subsequent day. At the end of every Sprint, an informal meeting is held wherein the Scrum team presents their progress and achievements to the stakeholders. This meeting is known as a Sprint review, and it helps the Scrum team obtain feedback from the stakeholders. The final event is the Sprint retrospective. This is a meeting when the Scrum team reviews the proceedings of the previous Sprint and comes up with ways in which improvements can be implemented for the upcoming Sprint.

Scrum Artifacts

There are two Scrum artifacts you must familiarize yourself with: the product backlog and the Sprint backlog. The product backlog is taken care of by the product owner. All the requirements desire from the viable product will be listed according to their priorities in the product backlog. It includes information about the different features, requirements, functions, any enhancements, and other fixes that showcase any changes required to be made to the product.

The Sprint backlog contains a detailed list of tasks as well as requirements that need to be attained during the subsequent Sprint. At times, a Scrum task board is also used for visualizing the progress of the tasks in the ongoing Sprint. Apart from this, any changes which are required to be made to the product are also listed on the Scrum task board using three different columns based on the status: to do, doing, and done.

Kanban

Kanban is a simple yet popular Agile methodology that focuses on the early release of products via collaboration between self-managing teams. It is quite similar to Scrum. The concept of Kanban was developed in the 1940s for optimizing the production line in the Toyota factories. Kanban offers the visual representation of the production process to deliver high-quality results by showing the workflow to determine any bottlenecks. The sooner the bottlenecks are identified in the workflow process, the easier it is to tackle them. Since any potential bottlenecks are identified during the early stages of the development process, it increases the overall efficiency. Six practices form the basis of Kanban:

- Visualization of the workflow

- Limiting the "work in progress" tasks

- Management of the workflow

- Explicitly stating all the policies

- Optimization and utilization of feedback loops

- Collaboration and experimental evolution of the processes

The visual cues used in a Kanban help identify the different stages of a developmental process. There are two key processes used in Kanban: the Kanban board and the Kanban cards. Apart from this, Kanban swimlanes can be used for a little extra organization.

The Kanban board helps visualize the developmental process. Either it can be a physical board, like sticky notes and a whiteboard, or a digital board. Digital boards are provided by different online project management tools like Zenkit. A Kanban card represents the item or task in progress. It helps communicate the workflow and progress to the team. It also determines vital information like the timeframe of the project, any upcoming deadlines, and the status of work. The Kanban swimlanes flow horizontally and provide for further classification of items via categorization. These swimlanes improve the overview of the work going on.

There are no specific rules you need to follow while using the Kanban project methodology. Use a Kanban board to visually represent the different stages of development starting from when the ideas were produced to ongoing work and finally the completion of work. Usually, the Kanban board is divided into three columns. The first column consists of all the tasks that need to be completed. The second column shows the work in progress, and the final one shows the completion of tasks. Kanban is quite popular in the software development industry. The flexibility it offers makes it the ideal choice in other industries, too. If a project requires any improvements during the development process, then Kanban will come in handy.

Lean

The lean management methodology helps minimize wastage while maximizing customer value. It is based on a simple principle that helps optimize the value a customer derives by reducing the use of resources. This management methodology was created in the Japanese manufacturing industry. The quality of the final output improves when waste is eliminated, and the costs, along with the production time, are reduced. Muda, Mura, and Muri are the three types of wastes identified by Lean methodology.

Any process that doesn't add any value to the project must be removed. Muda refers to this type of waste. Wastage can be of tangible and intangible resources. For instance, it can be a waste of physical resources or an intangible yet precious resource like time available. There are seven wastes identified by the Lean methodology:

- The transport or movement of a product between the locations and operations.

- Inventory or the work in progress along with any inventory of finished products and raw materials an organization maintains.

- Any physical movement made by a human being or a machine whenever an operation is conducted.

- Merely waiting for a product to arrive, for a machine to complete its task, or any other reason is a waste of time.

- Producing more than the demand or what the customer has ordered.

- Conducting unnecessary processes or operations that exceed the customer's requirements.

- Any defects in the form of product reject or rework required within the production process.

The removal of any variances in the workflow process during the scheduling and operational levels is known as Mura. The elimination of such variances helps ensure that everything goes along smoothly. For instance, if the editor of a magazine spends a long time editing an article, then the creative team will have less time for creating the spread before publishing the magazine. It might also mean that they won't have sufficient time to come up with the best possible spread because of the upcoming deadlines. Therefore, by reducing the time spent on editing, every department gets sufficient time to work on their aspect of the article while adhering to the deadline.

To ensure that nothing slows down during the production process, the team should remove some overloads. Muri is all about doing this. At times, business owners, as well as managers, tend to impose unnecessary stress on their processes and employees because of other factors like poor organizational structure, complicated working structure, or even using the wrong management tools. By reducing this overload, the production process can be streamlined, and the efficiency of the employees, along with their output, can be optimized.

Lean management places emphasis on following certain principles instead of implementing specific processes. There are five basic principles upon which the system is created:

- Specification of value by the final customer

- Identification of different steps in the value stream

- Ensuring a continuous product flow

- Enabling customers to pull value from the subsequent upstream activities

- Managing the work process while eliminating any unnecessary processes, steps, or activities.

Waterfall

The waterfall is a conventional project management methodology. It consists of linear and sequential design where progress flows downwards in a specific direction, almost like a waterfall. This technique first came up in the construction and manufacturing industries. It doesn't offer the flexibility of the other methods during the earlier stages of the development process, especially in the aspects related to design. Winston W. Royce came up with the Waterfall methodology in 1970; however, he didn't use the term "Waterfall." This technique essentially states that you cannot move from one phase of development to the next one until the current state is completed. There are six stages of development, and they are requirements of the system and the software, analysis, design, coding, testing, and operations.

This methodology emphasizes the importance of documentation throughout the process of development. It is based on the premise that even if one worker leaves during a development process, his or her replacement can easily start where the previous one left by using the information available in the different documents. It helps prevent any breaks in the flow of production, even if the workers change. Before Agile was introduced, the Waterfall management methodology was used in software development. However, the non-adaptive and rigid design constraints implemented by this methodology was quite challenging. Apart from this, the lack of a development process to obtain customer feedback, coupled with delays in the testing period, paved the way for newer management methodologies.

Six Sigma

The Six Sigma project management methodology was developed in 1986 by the engineers working at Motorola. The goal of this method is improving the quality of the final product by effectively reducing the errors in a process via identification of those things that aren't working and then eliminating them from the process altogether. Empirical and statistical quality management methods combined with the expertise of specialists in these methods are used in the Six Sigma project management methodology. Six Sigma green belts and six Sigma black belts are the two major methodologies within the Six Sigma, and they are both supervised by the Six Sigma Master Black Belts. The first methodology is DMAIC, and the second one is DMADV. The former is used to improve the efficiency of business processes, while the latter is used to create new processes, services, or products.

DMAIC stands for:

- Defining the problem along with the project goals

- Measuring the different aspects of the ongoing processes

- Analyzing all the data to identify any defects in a process

- Improving the efficiency of the project

- Controlling the way that the process will be executed in the future

DMADV stands for:

- Defining the project goals

- Measuring the critical components of a process along with the capabilities of the product

- Analyzing the data and developing different designs for a process and selecting the best from the lot

- Designing and testing the details of a process

- Verifying the design process by running it through simulations along with a pilot program and then handing the reins of the process to the client

Another method of Lean Six Sigma methodology is used to improve the performance of the team by strategically eliminating waste while reducing any variations in the process.

PMI/PMBOK

PMI or Project Management Institute is a non-profit membership association for project management certifications and standards of the organization. The PMI designed the PMBOK. Essentially, it isn't much of a methodology; instead, it is a set of guiding details for a set of standards that influence project management. Project Management Body of Knowledge or PMBOK is a set of standard guidelines and terminology for project management. According to the PMBOK, there are five process groups in every project:

Initiating

This is the stage where the group should define the start of a new phase in an existing project or the start of a new phase.

Planning

In the planning stage, the group should define the scope and objective of the project. Additionally, the group should also define how these objectives would be met.

Executing

In this phase, the group should work towards completing the steps or the processes defined in the plan.

Monitoring and Controlling

In this stage, the project manager will need to track, regulate, and review the performance and progress.

Closing

This is the final stage of the project, where the group will conclude the activities performed across all the process groups, and close the phase or project.

PMBOK also includes the best conventions, techniques, and practices that every team should adhere to. These guidelines are also updated regularly to ensure that they are up-to-date with the latest project management practices. In 2017, the PMBOK released its sixth edition.

When you begin working on a new project or phase in an existing project, you may want to apply many of the methodologies that were discussed in this chapter. This chapter only provides a guideline that you can use to help you select the right methodology for your project. Once you understand these methodologies better, you can perform further research to help you find the best match, and pair this up with a project management tool, like Zenkit.

Chapter Two: The Project Manager Role

Scott Berkun, the author of *Making Things Happen: Mastering Project Management*, stated that a project manager plays the role of a doctor in a team. A doctor leads the trauma team and chooses the procedure the team should perform on the patient. If there is nobody who can handle project management issues in the right way, the project can get into trouble. When do you think the role of a project manager came into existence? Microsoft was working on an ambitious project in the late 1980s, and this project had run into a problem. There were too many teams involved in the project, and they did not know how to coordinate with each other.

So, Microsoft decided to come up with an ingenious solution. They selected one person to take charge of the project. This person had the authority to coordinate the project and organize it. When Microsoft appointed a leader, the team could deliver the project smoothly, and the teams were happy with the dynamics. The result of this strategy was Excel. Microsoft eventually began to appoint someone to manage the project, and thus the role of a project manager was born.

Who Is a Project Manager?

A good project manager is someone with an excellent entrepreneurial mindset. This mindset gives them the necessary skills to not only manage the project but also manage the teams. A project manager can help the team meet the deadline and deliver the result. The success or failure of a project rests only on the project manager, and they are responsible for the result.

A project manager has the required information and knowledge to manage the project. They will need to understand the tasks that they assign to the team members and the technical know-how to ensure that the project moves forward. The latter skill does not only give the project manager the ability to communicate ideas to every person involved in the project but also helps them win the respect of the stakeholders and team members. Since a project manager will influence any of the decisions made in a project more than anybody else in the company, their task is to use all the knowledge they have to win their team members' respect.

Roles and Responsibilities of Project Managers

Resource and Activity Planning

The team and the project manager need to plan the project so they can meet the deadlines. Many projects fail because there was no planning. A good project manager will define the scope of the project and then determine if the resources are available. A good project manager will also know how to realistically set the time estimates and also evaluate the capabilities of the team. The project manager should then create a plan to complete the project and monitor the progress. A project is unpredictable, so a good project manager should know how to make the necessary adjustments to complete the project.

Motivating and Organizing the Team

A good project manager does not demotivate the team by giving them long checklists and elaborate spreadsheets to understand the progress of the project. Instead, they will always focus on their teams and put them in the center. They will work on a plan to enable their teams to meet their deadlines and reach their potential. They will work on removing bureaucracy and steer the team towards the goal.

Time Management

A client will always judge the success or failure of a project based on whether the team delivered the project on time or not. Therefore, it is important to understand that the timeline is non-negotiable. A good project manager knows how to set a realistic deadline for every task and also speak to the team regularly to understand the progress. They also know how to do the following:

- Maintain a schedule

- Define activity

- Estimate the duration of activity

- Sequence activity

- Develop a schedule

Estimating Cost and Developing the Budget

A good project manager knows how to stick to the budget allotted to the project. A project will be a failure if it goes over the budget, even if it is delivered on time and meets the expectations of the client. A good project manager will review the budget frequently and plan the tasks ahead to ensure that the team does not overrun the budget.

Ensuring Customer Satisfaction

A project is only successful when the customer is happy with the result. Every project manager is required to work towards avoiding any unwanted surprises, minimize uncertainty, and include their customers or clients in the project as much as possible. A good project manager is aware that they must communicate effectively with the customers and the business, and give them an update.

Identifying and Managing Project Risk

Regardless of how big or small a project, there will be obstacles, pitfalls, and hurdles that were not included as a part of the plan. A project manager will know how to identify, evaluate, and measure a potential risk before the project begins. They also make a note of the different ways to overcome that pitfall.

Monitoring Progress

During the start of the project, a project manager and his or her team should have a clear vision of the project. They will also hope to produce the desired output or result as per the timelines. This is, however, not always possible since the team will face some obstacles along the way. If things do not go according to the project plan, the project manager will need to monitor the progress, team performance, expenditure, and analyze that data to take corrective measures wherever required.

Managing Necessary Documentation and Reports

Experienced project managers know they need to maintain proper documentation and final reports for the project, and they know how to maintain this. A good project manager can present a comprehensive document that talks about how the team met all the requirements. This document should also provide some information on the history of the project, the team members involved, what tasks were done, and what can be done better in the future.

Do you need a Project Manager?

Regardless of how demanding or large a project is, you will need someone who can consistently and reliably maintain productivity and efficiency. Research shows that high-performing teams and organizations always have a project manager, and this is a profession that is consistently in demand. A project manager is indispensable to a successful project or business, and every business owner needs a leader who has the right skills, vision, and know-how to face any big challenges. These leaders are the only ones who can complete a project successfully and meet the timelines.

A project manager is an integral part of every organization, regardless of whether it is a small agency or a multinational company. The former only needs to hire one project manager, while the latter may need to hire many project managers or a highly-specialized project manager.

Chapter Three: Choosing the Right Methodology

You must choose the right project methodology to ensure that your team successfully delivers the project on budget and time. From Agile to waterfall to Kanban, there are numerous project management methodologies that you can choose from to maximize success.

This chapter will look at the different steps involved in choosing the right project management method based on the needs of the project and team. You must also ensure that the methodology will benefit your team and the project.

Benefits of Choosing an Organizational PM Method

One of the benefits is that these methods provide your team with guidelines, which will allow them to easily handle and establish different tasks in a project, including the budget, resources, timelines, stakeholders, and team members. There is no right way to handle a project. That being said, if you and your team assess the types of projects you work on along with the different components involved, you could make the right decision regarding the methodology. You can choose the one that will match the needs of your project.

It is difficult to choose the right approach to choosing a project management method since there are so many methods available to choose from. When you keep the project, objectives, and target goals in mind, you can choose the method and adapt it to cater to the needs of your project. Additionally, when you look at the pros and cons of different methods, you can choose numerous project management tools that will meet the requirements of your project.

Choosing the Right Method

You should choose the project management method based on the type of process or project that you work on. It is critical to choose the right project management based on some criteria since there are numerous methodologies or frameworks that you can choose from. Some criteria include:

- Scalability of project

- Project focus; for example, the objective or the different activities

- Allotted budget

- Specialization of roles

- Flexibility of timeline

- Stakeholder and customer involvement

- Industry

- Complexity of projects

- The different teams and the number of employees working on this project

- Resistance to change

- Maintaining an inventory of resources to identify those that are available and those that are needed

- Structure of the organization

- Selecting the dates for when the team starts and ends the project

Once you look at these components, you should identify the method that works best for you. Some of the steps included in this phase are:

>1. Since you have identified the goal or the objective of the project, you should look at the different variables that impact the tasks in the project. Weigh these variables against the objective or the goal of the project
>
>2. Identify the criteria on which the methodology will have an impact
>
>3. Assess the different methodologies and choose the method that is most relevant to the project
>
>4. Identify the advantages and disadvantages of every methodology and weigh them against each other
>
>5. Examine the methodology that will bring the most efficiency and success to your project, and also identify the project that will add more risk
>
>6. Collaborate with the team and weigh the decision
>
>7. Always document the method that you choose to implement
>
>8. Apply the methodology, and monitor the steps for the success and progress of that methodology

Software

When you have chosen the right method for your project, you must identify the right tool or software to implement that method. There are numerous options out there that will make it difficult for you to choose the right tool or software since there are many variables that you will need to consider. The following are some functionalities to consider when you need to choose the right project management software for your project.

Gantt Charts

Project managers and businesses use Gantt charts to look at the amount of work done. These charts depict the tasks completed in the form of a series of horizontal lines on the chart. You can also use this chart to represent the targets hit during specific times in the project. This view will help you look at the time that the team took to complete a task in comparison to the time that the team was supposed to take as per the plan. This functionality is often used when the waterfall project management method is applied to a project since the team should adhere to a strict timeline.

Kanban Boards

Kanban boards are workflow visualization tools that allow project managers and teams to optimize the workflow. They use these boards to see how the project is progressing. You can use a Kanban board to communicate progress reports, status updates, project issues, and more, thereby offering your team full visibility of the project. The Kanban board is often paired with the Kanban methodology, where the teams are required to focus only on working on the tasks and deliver the tasks and projects over a fluid timeline. These boards are also used in the Lean project management method to allocate tasks to team members and also manage the inventory and resources.

Calendars

You can use a calendar to show the stakeholders and the business a detailed view of the project timelines. You can also show them the dates of completion. This gives the team members, stakeholders, businesses, and customers complete visibility of the status of the project. This view is often used in project methodologies like Scrum and XPM (Extreme Programming).

Mobile Accessibility

When customers and team members can view the status of the project—including the tasks completed, the progress, changes in the timeline, and more—on their mobile device, it is considered important in the overall success of the project. It is easier to use this tool when you use a project management methodology that is fluid. You can also use it when the project has different parts with some dependencies, like Agile.

Cross-Project Summary Views

A cross-project view will give the departments and teams involved in the project a full insight into the development of the project. This feature makes it easier for you to share real-time status updates, dashboards, and roll-up checkpoint details that will give customers, stakeholders, and the team members an update throughout the project. It is best to use this feature with methodologies that require some updates due to the fluid-structure, like Scrum, Agile, and XPM. Having said that, it could be used for other methodologies, too.

PART TWO: Lean Project Management

Chapter Four: What Is Lean?

As mentioned earlier, one of the core principles of Lean is to maximize customer value and minimize waste. In simple words, lean helps to provide customers with a product of greater value using fewer resources. Lean thinking will make the organization focus on those processes that require a change. The management will learn to focus on how the flow of products and services can be optimized horizontally across assets, technology, and departments to its customers instead of focusing on separate technology, vertical departments, and assets.

The management will also have to look at how the processes that add waste to the project should be removed along the value stream. The business needs to look at how the processes should be optimized to reduce human effort, human time, capital, and space. This will help to reduce the cost incurred to finish the product or service. These companies find it easier to meet the changing needs of their customers with high-quality products, great variety, faster delivery, and low cost. Information management will also become more accurate and straightforward.

Lean Management for Production and Services

Most people believe that lean management only works in the manufacturing department, and this is not true. The Lean management methodology can be applied to different types of processes and businesses. It is not a method that is used only to reduce the cost. This methodology gives businesses a set of principles to improve the way the business thinks or acts. Businesses in different industries and sectors, including healthcare and government, have begun to use lean principles to change the way the processes function in the business. Companies that move away from traditional practices and approaches to a lean way of thinking are undergoing a lean transformation. James Womack, Ph.D., who led a research team at an International Motor Vehicle Program at MIT describing Toyota's business, coined the term lean in the late 1980s.

Lean Business Principles

The book *Lean Thinking: Banish Waste and Create Wealth in Your Corporation* introduced the American Business Market to lean business principled in the early 1990s. Lean thinking originated in the manufacturing models in Toyota automotive in the late 1980s following the introduction of Kanban. Different businesses and industries now use lean business models and principles to reduce time spent on delivering high-quality products and reducing the number of resources used to achieve that goal. Some principles of lean business models will now be detailed.

Perfection

It is important for a business to continually refine the first four principles to ensure that processes have minimal or no waste in them. The idea behind this principle is that any waste that goes unnoticed in the first four stages is always exposed over time. It is important to eliminate that waste to help a business adapt to the changing needs of its customers.

Peter Hines has argued that the five principles of lean thinking may be insufficient for some or most contemporary business situations. He stated that businesses need to apply lean thinking only to some processes like order fulfillment without giving any regard to communication, leadership, or quality management. Therefore, it is essential to understand how lean thinking can be applied to help a business develop a holistic approach to the delivery of products and services.

Value Identification

Every business and team must bear in mind that the value of any company will only lie with the customers or stakeholders. Every company should strive to meet the customers' demands. If the customer requires a specific product, the business must work on identifying the right resources to complete that job. Every business needs to understand the customers' needs and identify the products or services that will cater to those needs.

Value Stream Mapping

Once the business defines the products or services that it should provide to the customers, the management needs to map the different processes that the teams will need to complete to deliver that product or service. The business can identify the different steps included in the project during the mapping process. Businesses can also identify the steps that do not add any value to the project and eliminate those. For instance, if the business discovers the process to place orders by employees is complicated, it must eliminate that process since it is a waste contributor.

Flow

As mentioned earlier, the business can identify the various steps that do not add any value to the processes during the mapping step. The business should then work on removing those processes from the system. This will ensure that there are no obstacles in the business, and the product or service can be delivered to the customer with fewer hiccups. For instance, if a gardening service must visit an off-site location to stock up on supplies, it will take a longer time to deliver its services. The business should try to identify whether they can afford to increase the on-site storage space.

Pull

Lean processes always produce the output based on the demand of the customers, which makes these processes "pull processes". A pulled process is one where the call for the production of a product or service is on an as-needed or as-wanted basis. In service businesses, the delivery is always dependent on the workforce. For example, a pizza delivery service can choose to hire delivery executives based on the demand for pizza. If it is the football season, more customers are bound to order pizzas, and it is a good idea for the business to hire more executives to deliver the pizza.

Lean Tools

Lean companies use the support of different tools and processes to support the principles of lean. These tools help the business identify the processes that do not add value to the business and remove those processes. This chapter lists some of the tools that you can use to implement lean in your business.

Takt Time

Lean businesses should always look for different methods to optimize processes. This is the only way the business can ensure that they satisfy the demands of their stakeholders or customers. Takt time is the average rate at which a team or business produces the output based on the customer's requirement and in the stipulated time.

Takt = (Time available to produce a product or service) / (Demands made by the customer)

Continuous Flow

This tool ensures that the batch size is reduced to eliminate some constraints in the system. The business must identify a method by which it produces products or information that moves at a consistent pace from one step that adds value to the next with zero delays or waste in between.

Standardized Work

The business should create a document that will list the processes or methods that the organization uses to produce the goods and services to meet the calculated takt time. This document will enable the business to standardize the tasks and improve the value of the workstream.

Kanban and Pull Systems

As you read earlier, Kanban is a project management methodology that allows the project manager and the teams to schedule tasks. It also sheds some light on the different processes that every department must complete to obtain the result. This tool was developed by Taiichi Ohno to improve the manufacturing process of Toyota automotive in the late 1980s.

Cellular Manufacturing

Cellular marketing will aim to reduce the time it takes for the business to meet the demand of the customer or market, and allow the business to identify the processes that reduce the time taken to deliver the necessary output. Workstations and equipment are arranged to bring different teams to manufacture similar products.

The Why's

It is important for a business always to question the problem and identify the cause of any problem that may arise in the process. For instance, if there is a delay in the supply of the raw material, the business should ask the following questions:

- Why is there no backup supplier?

- Why are we sticking to this supplier only?

Level the Workload

Customer patterns always vary in the business, and the processes in the business are always consistent. This means that the processes in the business can only cater to handling specific customer patterns. Businesses need to identify the different patterns and plan the workflow based on these patterns.

Problem Solving

Most businesses or teams adopting the lean project management method adopt the PDCA cycle. This cycle is a graphical and logical representation of how individuals in the company identify problems and solve them. This will allow the company to view the process at a granular level.

- Plan: Establish the plan to achieve the final goal

- Do: Implement the plan

- Check: Collect, collate, and analyze the results

- Act: Implement reforms only if the business is unable to obtain the desired results

The business can now work on developing a system that will help the employees identify the problems and solve them by identifying the cause of the problem. The business can also work on implementing some countermeasures that will eliminate the problem.

Chapter Five: Start a Lean Project

Now that you understand what the Lean methodology is, now look at how you can implement lean project management at work. You can implement lean methodology using the phases below:

- Initiation

- Planning

- Execution

- Monitoring and Control

- Closing

Initiation

Before you begin a project, you should work on defining the value or the objective of the project during the project initiation phase. This project charter will specify the value of the project and also the items of value that the team should produce at the end of the project. This project charter will define the project requirements, including the quality standards, support requirements, interim deliverables, and maintenance required for project success.

Planning

It is during the planning phase that the project manager will define the value steam and map that value stream to different tasks. When it comes to lean project management, it is a good idea to use a work breakdown structure (WBS) to create the value stream map since this identifies the different steps that the team will take to complete the project. Lean project management will develop a schedule that will specify the timeline for the entire project.

Execution

The lean project management excels in execution. The project execution phase of lean management will include the following steps:

Flow

Once the tasks enter the production process, the goods being produced—like information products, tangible goods, services, etc.—do not stop moving. For a project that does not require full-time work, the project manager and team should work together to identify and document the set of partial deliverables at regular intervals. For instance:

- In an engineering project, the specifications and plans should be produced using the takt time as a criterion

- In a construction project, the tradespeople will line up and work on tasks without any gaps

- In a software development project, the functionality will be demonstrated using a continuous cycle, daily, monthly or whatever timeline suits the project better

- In a training project, the material must be produced at a measurement that works best for the team

Inventory

The lean methodology helps to minimize the inventory being used. This will ensure that the product delivered to the customer is better than what was expected. If there is a task that the team can complete without any additional inputs, the work can be completed and delivered to the customer. For example:

- In an engineering project, every specification and drawing will be certified as complete without having to wait for the other specification and drawing

- In a construction project, team members should complete the tasks and the project and also accept the ownership of that task at some point during the cycle

- In a software development project, the owner of the task is given the authority to take care of product functionality for the acceptance in the stages instead of the entire product

Kaizen

The lean process is managed continuously to identify waste or any other process or task that does not add value to the project. In this stage, the project manager should monitor the work breakdown structure to look at the scope.

Monitoring & Control

Every team member working as part of a lean team has the authority to push the red button or stop any process if they notice a problem with the quality. This task will stop the minute the issue has been identified, and a solution is found. Every individual project or completed task will be given this treatment. The team will not move to the next task until the completed task meets the specified quality standards.

Lean project management will use jidoka, a lean concept, where the quality of the product is checked at every stage of the process, and any issues in quality are identified and rectified immediately. It is also acceptable for the team to stop working on any other task until the completed output meets the quality standards. Therefore, every task in a project is defined as complete using human judgment.

Closing

Lean project management will seek to hand the deliverables over to the customer very quickly. The team will factor in dates when they can deliver partial deliverables to customers at an earlier date to understand whether the stakeholders will accept the product or not.

Chapter Six: Lean Six Sigma

Lean and Six Sigma are different approaches, but they can be combined because they have some similarities that allow them to work well together. The differences ensure that there are some analytical solutions and tools that will help to improve the process, service, or product. It is because of these similarities that both lean and six sigma analysis can be performed on the same process, service, or product.

Similarities of Lean and Six Sigma

The similarities of these methods:

> • Both methods rely on the definition of the value, which is based on the experience of the customer. The customer is the boss.

> • Both these methods use a process flow mapping approach, which will enable them to understand the process better. Even if the analysis is only based on a process, product, or service, there is another process that will be associated with creating and delivering the service or product.

- The methods rely on the data, which is used to determine the current performance and also for determining the impact of the processes on the future performance of the business. The data collected from a Lean Six Sigma project can be used in both the Six Sigma and Lean analysis. The reliance of these analysis methods on the data will help to ensure that the cause of the problem is defined.

- Both methods are applied to projects that include cross-functional teams. The size of the team and the duration of the project will depend solely on the scale and scope of the process, service, or product that is currently being analyzed for the improvement.

- These methods were earlier used only on the manufacturing operation, but it can be used for all functions in the business. These methods can also be used for internally and externally facing processes. They are also used in different industries, including consumer, industrial, non-profit, education, and government.

- Any improvement made to the processes using either approach will reduce variation and will also reduce waste. Removing any waste steps and activities will help to remove numerous sources of variation. When you remove variation, you can remove the wasted process steps and capacity.

There are, however, some differences in these approaches. These differences will not create a conflict, but they will provide multiple paths that can be used to arrive at the same destination. A lean six sigma project will always identify the defect defined by the customer and dictate the appropriate tools to cater to that defect. The final solution is obtained as a combination of both Six Sigma and lean improvements.

What is the Difference between Lean and Six Sigma?

Now that you know what the similarities are, look at some of the differences between these methods:

1. Both methods focus on different aspects of the problem. Six sigma focuses primarily on reducing variation, which means that the processes will always need to work towards meeting the target performance levels, while lean focuses primarily on waste.

2. Each of these methods implements different techniques. Lean uses visual techniques to identify the solution and analyze the progress. The solution is derived from the data collected during the analysis. Six Sigma uses statistical techniques to analyze and identify the right solution by using data visualization. This will lead to the assumption that it is easier to use lean over six sigma since the visual analysis is easier to understand. People are often intimidated by the Six Sigma analysis. The truth is that both these analyses are easy to understand and perform with the statistical tools that are present today.

3. Different types of documentation are present to obtain a solution. The lean solution uses a value stream map that will address the changes in the workflow. If you follow the lean methodology, you should maintain a document that will provide instructions on the many steps in the process. The six sigma solution focuses on changing the setup procedures. It also talks about how to monitor the process and respond to any variation in the process. The changes will also impact the instructions and also lead to some changes in the measurement systems or approaches.

Both these approaches are complementary in many ways, and it is easy to merge them into one methodology. Lean Six Sigma will avoid the issues of the earlier approaches.

Lean Six Sigma principles

Some principles of lean six sigma, which makes the methodology effective, will now be detailed. There are many other principles of this methodology, but the ones listed in this section have always led to successful programs.

Addressing a Real-World Problem

Lean six sigma is both a bottom-up and top-down approach or methodology. The latter is associated with the selection of the problem. Most teams work on real-world problems that impact different processes and customers. When it comes to lean processes or any process in general, the team members have to collectively work on reworking or revising the output based on customer feedback. This will make it hard for the team members to focus on the other parts of the project. This will lead to a sense of urgency when it comes to completing specific tasks. It is important to understand that this is real work.

There was a program called Quality Circle that was adopted by many companies in the year 1980. In this program, teams in an organization were allowed to choose their projects. This does sound great since it empowers the employees, but there was an issue with the projects selected by these teams. Most teams did not choose real-world problems. Some teams may choose trivial problems like putting up curtains in the lunchroom or repainting the office. Teams viewed this initiative as a fun initiative and did not worry about improving the business.

It is hard to make businesses and teams understand the importance of this method, which makes it difficult for most businesses to succeed in using this method. It is easy to convince teams to adopt this method if they understand why it is important for them to identify the problem and work on a solution to fix that problem. The management should not define both the problem and the solution. The teams should analyze the problem and determine the cause.

A Team Accomplishes Analysis

Lean six sigma teams often have members with different capabilities, and each of the members is given a different problem to analyze. Business processes are often cross-functional, and teams must perform cross-functional analysis to optimize and improve the process. It does not make sense to improve one step at the expense of other steps. This does not remove any variation or waste, and it just shifts the focus to a different step in the process.

Some issues arise with the lean six sigma approach since employees with the Green and Black belts often chose to identify the problem and also develop the solution to that problem without taking the inputs from the other team members. This would be an effective method if the teams were very small, and the project manager and other team members understood the entire process. This method, however, will not work for cross-functional teams and projects. If the project leader or manager is determined to identify the problem or solution without the help of other team members, and he or she does not know what the problem is, the project will be delayed.

When you include a cross-functional team, the perspective of every department in the organization is involved. These teams will collectively work together to understand the problem and develop the solution to the problem. Every member of the team must have a clear understanding of the problem. The problem must be looked at from different perspectives since that will help the team develop a solution that will address the issue immediately. This solution will also eliminate variation and waste in the other steps in the process.

The Analysis is Focused on a Process

Lean six sigma is an approach that one can use to analyze processes. This approach is more effective when it is applied to processes that either build or design products instead of looking only at the product, even if the problem is a product problem. Most businesses use the lean six sigma analysis of the "improve or investigate" processes and actions. Actions or tasks are a part of the process, and teams can complete most of these tasks without worrying about whether they are preceding or succeeding tasks. The teams should only focus on the context in which these tasks occur in the process. You can use the Six Sigma process map or lean value stream map to obtain a picture of that process.

Experts say that a process map helps teams immediately understand what is happening in the project. These maps also help teams recognize the problems in the process, which are often hidden since only an individual is aware of the task that he or she is performing. Your customers can come back with feedback about a defect in the product, which means that the team must rework on the product and fix that defect. Instead of focusing on the process that was followed to develop the product, the teams focus only on the defect. This is where they make a mistake since the team could identify the defect in the product, but they could not identify the cause of the problem. Teams can only do this when they define a process map and identify the problem.

The Analysis is Based on Data

Lean six sigma focuses only on data and not intuition. The value stream map will have a list of all the steps in the process, and the team collects data at every step. It is during the measure phase that the current condition of the product, service, and process is calculated. In this phase, the team should measure the defect or problem and measure whether the steps are being followed correctly. The data collected will help the team, and the project manager determines the actual state of the problem. This analysis will help teams identify the underlying causes of the problem and correct that problem. This is not where the teams stop relying on the data. Once the team identifies the solution, the team should collect data to assess whether the solution has fixed the problem or not. Once the data confirm that the solution works, the team should continue to collect data to ensure that the problem does not return.

One of the main challenges that most teams have with problem-solving initiatives and continuous improvement is that they are unable to accept the current conditions. Most businesses are in denial about many issues and problems in the company. Look at an example: There is a process in a company that is working on resolving any product issues that created large levels of rework for the team because there were numerous complaints from the customer. The business worked on solving the issue by fixing the problem with the product on many occasions by identifying the task that led to the defect. The team did identify the problem, but the issue here was that the team did not look at all the other steps in the process. If the team paid better attention to the data collected from the processes, the members would have identified that there was more than one task that led to the defect in the product. It is important to ensure that the data is fully understood and looked at correctly.

Understand the Impact of the Process Sigma

This principle focuses on the use of the six sigma analysis. Sigma is a statistical term that represents the variation that occurs from the normal values in the business. It is tied to the characteristics of the parameter that the business uses to measure success. There will be no variation between the same attributes of a process or product. Regardless of the number of times this process or product occurs, the attribute will not change. There will be some variations in other attributes. There will be an average value and some uncertainty assigned to the occurrence of some instances. Sigma represents uncertainty.

- One sigma is used to represent the boundaries of uncertainty for two-thirds of the occurrences

- Two sigmas are used to represent the confidence interval for 95 percent of the occurrences

- Three sigmas are used to represent the confidence interval for 99 percent of the instances

- When you reach the six sigma figure, you will note that there are only three occurrences out of a million that the normal variation can make a change to the product or output

It is important to understand that sigma only talks about variation and not acceptability. If you read the paragraph above, you will notice that it is not talking about assessing whether the customer accepted the product or not. The attribute in question can have a very small value for sigma, which means that there is no variation. That said, if the mean or average value of that attribute is out of the acceptable bounds for a customer, the product or output is defective. If the attribute has a high sigma value, it means that there is high uncertainty associated with that variable. If the customer does not have any expectations from that attribute, the product will still be accepted.

The Lean Six Sigma project management methodology does not use the sigma value to assess customer acceptance. It looks at how to accommodate for any high variations in the attributes. You need to understand that your output is generated through a process. When there are processes with high variation and high uncertainty, the business will need to spend more time and money to assess the process. You must remember that you are following a process, and the outputs of the previous step become the inputs of the next step. If there is too much variation in the input variable, it is important to develop the process in a way that the consecutive steps can accommodate different possibilities and values for those inputs. This will add some complexity to the processes. When you lower the sigma level, you can simplify the entire process.

The Solution Addresses the Real Root Cause(s)

Lean Six Sigma is one of the most common and powerful continuous improvement and problem-solving methodologies since it will identify the different characteristics of the actual problem. Some methodologies look at the problem from a single point of view. They will identify the problem, look for the cause, and develop a solution to address that problem. These methodologies work on the assumption that the solution will eliminate the entire problem. Other methodologies work on the assumption that the problem occurs in almost every process, and it occurs very often. The process is inadequate or flawed, and a change to the process will eliminate the problem.

The goals of both these types of methodologies are similar and quite admirable. The way to fix the issue in the first method is to place a correction in the process to control the cause. In the second method, the entire process will be reengineered. This does not improve the situation and often makes the situation worse. Lean Six Sigma uses different tools to identify the problem and assess if the problem is a common cause or if it is a special case. Once this differentiation is made, the team can work on identifying the cause of the problem and address that problem appropriately. The team can develop a solution strategy to address the problem. The team can implement a simple solution if the problem is a special cause. If the problem is common, the team can work on redesigning the process.

Benefits of Lean Six Sigma

Lean Six Sigma, like lean, is a continuous improvement approach or methodology. It is, however, important to understand how this method improves processes. Does this method increase profits or sales? Does it reduce the number of complaints from customers, or does it improve customer satisfaction? Does it lower the costs, improve the quality of the raw material or the product, or lower the cost of quality? Does the process improve employee morale? Can you use this process to promote your products and services? Does it increase benefits and pay? Well, yes. Now, look at some benefits of the Lean Six Sigma methodology for a business and an individual.

Organizational Benefits

Since lean six sigma is a continuous improvement framework or methodology, an organization is bound to benefit from this method. General Electric (GE) claims that the lean six sigma methodology has helped the company save over $2 billion. Look at some of the benefits of this method and its implications.

Simple Processes

Lean six sigma will help businesses and teams simplify numerous processes. Since the methodology focuses on a cross-functional approach, the value stream maps will help the organization identify the inefficiencies and waste in different parts of the process. Many processes will embed workarounds and rework to cater to persistent problems. If the team can identify these workarounds or areas where there is a lot of rework, they can remove the waste, which will then make the process easier to control and manage. This will lead to the creation of a faster process, which will then lead to higher customer satisfaction and better customer service, thereby increasing sales. Additionally, faster processes will reduce any overhead costs, thereby increasing profits. Simpler processes have fewer errors, and it is for this reason that fewer defects and higher quality characterize these processes.

Fewer Errors and Mistakes

Now dig a little deeper into this benefit. The Lean Six Sigma methodology defines the quality of the product based on what the customer values. When businesses focus on improving processes to meet the external requirements, they will address those problems that have an impact on the success of the business. The teams must use the data collected at every step and use that data to improve some real problems in the organization. So, the Lean Six Sigma method does not just cater to improving processes with mistakes or errors but also focuses on improving the processes that matter most to the business.

Predictable Performance

It is easy to manage and control simple processes when compared to complex processes. In addition to the above benefits, Lean Six Sigma also focuses on removing any variation in the processes, thereby making the processes predictable. This means that the teams can predict the cycle time, costs, and quality of the output. This level of predictability will lead to higher profits, better customer service, and fewer complaints. Organizations that have this level of predictability can work well in an environment where the changes are fast-moving. Changes in customer expectations and technology will create an unstable business environment. If you do not have predictable processes in the business, it will be impossible to develop a solution to cater to this instability.

Active Control

The Lean Six Sigma approach can help businesses and teams actively control the processes. The methodology reduces the cycle times and uses real-time data to analyze these cycles allowing the businesses to develop real-time data systems and control plans. Process managers and operators can make the right decisions that directly impact the performance of the processes. This will improve employee morale, agility, and performance. An operator should understand how their work improves or impacts the performance of the process. The lean six sigma approach gives the operator immediate feedback. Since the operators working on the task are given control of these processes, they do not feel like the victims. With active control and short cycles, an organization can respond to the changing markets and grab new opportunities.

Personal Benefits

You, as an individual, can reap the benefits of lean six sigma within an organization. Now, look at some of the benefits of lean six sigma that you, as an individual, can expect when you work in an organization that participates in lean six sigma.

Personal Effectiveness

The lean six sigma project management methodology is a problem-solving methodology that can be used to address problems of different kinds. Your ability to perform in any industry or position in the business will improve if you learn how to identify and fix some problems. The lean six sigma project management method will steer you through an organized process of analysis, problem identification, inquiry, and solution creation. You can apply numerous tools and techniques to some of the common issues and problems. Even if you do not want to use all the tools that are available to you, you can use the lean six sigma approach to control the processes and identify the problem. You can use this method to solve issues in different business settings.

Leadership Opportunity

The lean six sigma project management methodology is implemented through numerous projects, and each of these projects has a different leader. When you lead a lean six sigma project, you will have the opportunity to look at different functions and speak to the senior management. This exposure will help you develop the abilities to identify a problem and also come up with a solution to fix that problem. When you interact with managers and team members, you can improve your decision-making skills and communication. The structure of the lean six sigma model will help you develop and work on your project management skills. You can seek the next opportunity or a promotion if you can put it on your résumé that you led a project that improved quality, saved costs, and also reduced the time taken to complete the project.

Industries and Functions using Lean Six Sigma

The lean project management methodology was first used in the engineering department by an automotive manufacturer. The Six Sigma project management methodology was first used in the quality department of a technology system manufacturer. These methodologies, however, have moved beyond these industries and departments. The lean six sigma project management methodology can be used in different departments, including:

- C-Suite

- Call Center

- Customer Service

- Design Engineering
- Field Sales
- Finance
- Human Resources
- IT
- Legal
- Logistics
- Maintenance
- Manufacturing Engineering
- Manufacturing Operations
- Marketing
- Process Engineering
- Purchasing/Sourcing
- Quality
- R&D
- Sales
- Test

The lean project management methodology has moved beyond the realm of manufacturing, and many businesses in different industries have begun to implement lean six sigma in their business processes. In some cases, the business may focus more on six sigma or lean, but many businesses focus on a combination of lean and six sigma.

- Agri-business
- Aviation
- Banking
- Electronics

- Financial Services
- Government
- Higher Education
- Hospitals
- Manufacturing
- Medical Devices
- Mining
- Oil and Gas
- Pharmaceuticals
- Retail
- Telecom
- Transportation

Chapter Seven: Lean Startup

Eric Ries said that startups could be a success if they follow a certain process. This means that the process can always be learned, and those who have experience can also teach them. Every entrepreneur will always wonder whether a startup will fail.

If you wish to begin a lean startup, you must identify a small gap in the market using time and money effectively. You will need to use different techniques to ensure that your product or service reaches the market in a faster way while also avoiding the production or manufacture of products that no consumer will want.

Most amateur entrepreneurs feel that they are taking a shot in the dark when they are identifying a product or service they can offer to their potential consumers. However, it does not always have to be a trial and error proposition. If you adopt lean thinking, you will be able to develop ideas and refine them to meet market standards.

The following are some principles that will give a startup a greater chance of making a profit and becoming a success within a limited budget.

Principles of Lean Startup

Validated Learning

A startup does not exist only to build products for the customers or to make money. It also can only exist when the management learns how to build a sustainable business. The learning can be validated through statistic measures by running experiments that test the startup's vision.

Entrepreneurs are Everywhere

Eric Ries believes that every individual in the world is an entrepreneur. Some successful entrepreneurs have built their organization in their garage. You can find entrepreneurs in Hollywood, in the IRS, and even in well-established organizations. These people are always looking for a way to develop products that increase value to the customer.

Controlled Use and Deployment of Resources

One of the most important principles of a lean startup is that the startup must use every one of its resources effectively and efficiently. Since most startups do not have enough investment, they use the lean business model to encourage the effective deployment and continuous development of the resources that the company does have.

A lean startup must continuously evaluate how the initial investment can be used to meet its targets and customer requirements. The startup must also ensure that it does not spend more than what is necessary to test, evaluate, and refine its products. If the costs are kept at a minimum, the startup can maximize its profits whenever there is a sale.

Every lean startup is dependent on organic growth since it does not have a huge capital investment. When the profits made at the early stages are reinvested in the company, the startup can scale its operations up in a controlled manner without sacrificing quality. This is commonly called innovation accounting.

Innovation Accounting

A startup must focus on the following to improve outcomes and also hold every entrepreneur accountable:

- How can progress be measured

- How can milestones be set

- How can work be prioritized

Entrepreneurship is Management

It is important to remember that every startup is not defined by its products but is an institution. Therefore, there must be a management team in place to understand and develop the startup.

Build-Measure-Learn

Every startup looks for ways to convert its ideas into a product or service and measure how its customers receive that product or service. When they understand the response, they will understand whether they need to pivot or persevere. This process is covered in further detail in the next chapter.

Models and Methodologies

The lean startup model was introduced in 2011, and its impact on the economy has been enormous. The book written by Eric Ries gained immense publicity, and many companies use the information in the book to develop their startups. However, the ideas in the book are not new; most entrepreneurs have forgotten these ideas since success is always measured in numbers in the business world. The methods and ideas in the book are valuable to startups as well as well-established organizations. In his book, Eric Ries has defined a startup as a human institution whose goal is to create a new service or product under uncertain conditions. This chapter covers some of the common methods used by lean startups to design products and services of great value for the customer.

Build-Measure-Learn

The way different companies pursue innovation in today's market has been affected by the idea of using certain scientific or statistical methods to handle or calculate uncertainty. This means that the company must define a hypothesis, build a product or service to test that hypothesis, use that product or service and learn what happens, and finally adjust the attributes of the product or service to increase the value for customers.

The Build-Measure-Learn methodology can be applied to almost anything. You do not have to use this methodology to test new products alone. You can also test a management review process, customer service idea, new features to existing products or website offers, and tests. You have to carry out a test and validate the initial hypothesis to ensure that you have enough data to assess the value of the product to the customer.

The aim of every company should be to move through this methodology quickly. You have to identify if the product or service developed is worth going through another cycle or if you should come up with a new idea. This means that you must define a specific idea that you want to test with minimum criteria that can be used for measurement. When it comes to products, you have to test whether your customers want to purchase your product or if they need it. You have to learn what your customers want and not trust what they think or say they want.

Minimal Viable Product (MVP)

A traditional company will first have to define the specifications of every product it wants to produce or manufacture and then assess the high cost and time that will be invested to produce that product. The lean startup methodology encourages every startup to build the required amount of product through one loop of the Build-Measure-Learn loop. If the company can identify such a product, it becomes a minimal viable product. This product is manufactured or developed using minimal effort and less development time.

Every startup does not necessarily have to write a code to automate processes to create an MVP. An MVP could be as simple as a slide deck or design mockups. You have to ensure that you run these products by your customers to get enough validation to pass this product through the next cycle.

Validated Learning

Every startup must test or validate a hypothesis with the right idea in mind—learn from what is observed. There are times when startups have focused on vanity metrics that made them believe that they were indeed making progress. This is not the right approach since you must always look at metrics that will give you some insight on the product and how it can be changed to increase its value to the customers. For example, the number of accounts opened on Instagram is a vanity metric for that platform. The actual metric would be the number of hours spent scrolling through Instagram by each account holder. This will give the developers the true value of the product.

In the book Lean Startup, Eric Ries has provided an example of his own. A company called IMVU always showed a chart that painted a good picture of its management and investors. Many registrations were being made every single day. However, this graph did not show if the customers or users value the service. The graph did not show the costs that went into marketing to acquire new users. This chart only looked at vanity metrics and was not designed to test a hypothesis.

Innovation Accounting

Through innovation accounting, a startup can prove that it is learning to grow and sustain itself as a business. A company can do this in the following ways.

Establish a Baseline

The startup can run an MVP test and collect data that will enable it to set some benchmark points. You can use a smoke test where you can market the product or service you want to offer and assess your customers' interests. This includes a sign-up form to understand if the customers want to purchase the product or service. Using that information, you can set the baseline for the first iteration of the Build-Measure-Learn cycle. It is all right to make mistakes or have low numbers since that will help you improve.

Tuning the Product

Once the baseline has been established, you should identify one change that must be made to the product and test that improvement. Do not make all the changes at once, as it can lead to chaos. You can try to see how a change in the design of the form attracts more customers when compared to the earlier design. This step must be carried out slowly to ensure that every hypothesis is tested out carefully.

Persevere or Pivot

When you have made several iterations through the cycle, you have to move up from the initial baseline towards the goal that was set out in the business plan. If you are unable to reach that goal, you must learn why using the data collected at every step.

Pivot

A successful entrepreneur is one who has the foresight, the tools, and the ability to identify which parts of the business plan are indeed working for the company. They also learn to adapt to changes in the market and their strategies according to the data collected during the iterations.

One of the hardest aspects of the lean startup method is to decide to pivot since every entrepreneur and founder is emotionally attached to the product they have created. They spend a lot of money and energy to get to where they are. If a team uses vanity metrics to test its products and hypothesis, it can go down the wrong path. If the hypothesis selected is not defined clearly, then the company may fail since the management does not know that the endeavor is not working. If you, as the management, decide to launch the product fully in the market and then assess the outcome, you will see what happens, and there is a higher probability that you may fail.

If you choose to pivot, it does not mean that you have failed. It means that you will change the hypothesis that you started with. The following variations are often used when a startup chooses to pivot.

- Zoom-in Pivot: A single feature in the product that sets it apart from other products becomes the actual product.

- Zoom-out pivot: This is the opposite of the above definition, where an entire product is used as a new feature in a larger product.

- Customer segment pivot: The product designed was correct. However, the customers that were selected were wrong for the product. The startup can change the customer segment and sell the same product.

- Customer need pivot: When the startup follows the principles of validated learning, it will identify the problem that needs to be solved for the customer who was initially selected.

- Platform pivot: Most platforms start as applications. When the platform becomes a success, it transforms into a platform ecosystem.

- Business Architecture Pivot: Based on Geoffrey Moore's idea, the startup can choose to switch to low margin and high-volume products from the high margin and low-value products.

- Value Capture Pivot: When you decide to measure the value differently, you will be able to change everything about the business right from the cost structure to the final product.

- The engine of Growth Pivot: According to Ries, most startups follow a paid, viral, or sticky growth model. It would be more prudent for the company to switch from one model to the other to grow faster.

- Channel Pivot: In today's world, advertising channels and complex sales have reduced since the Internet provides a huge platform for a company to advertise its products.

- Technology Pivot: Technological advancements are being made every day, and any new technology can help to reduce the cost and increase performance and efficiency.

Small Batches

There is a story where a father had asked his daughters to help him stuff newsletters into a document. The children suggested that they fold every newsletter, put a stamp on the envelope, and write the address on the envelope. They wanted to do every task one step at a time. The father wanted to do it differently—he suggested that they finish every envelope before they moved on to the next envelope. The father and daughters competed with each other to see which the better method was.

The father's method won since he used an approach called "single-piece flow", which is common in lean manufacturing. It is better to repeat a task over and over again to ensure that you master that task. You will also learn to do the task faster and better. You have to remember that an individual's performance is not as important as the performance of the system. You lose time when you should go back to the first task and restack the envelopes. If you consider the process as a unit, you can improve your efficiency.

Another benefit of using small batches is that you will be able to spot the error immediately. If you fold all the newsletters and then find out that that newsletter does not fit into the envelope, you will need to fold all the newsletters again. This approach will help you identify the error at the beginning and improve your process.

The advantage of working with small batches is that you will be able to identify the problems soon.

Andon Cord

The Andon Cord is a method that was used by Taiichi Ohno in Toyota, which allowed an employee to stop the process if he or she identified a defect in the process. If the defect continues longer in the process, it is harder to remove that defect, and there is a higher cost involved. It is highly efficient to spot the defect at an early stage, even if it means that the process will need to stop to address the defect. This method has helped Toyota maintain high quality.

Eric Ries mentioned in his book that the company IMVU used a set of checks that ran every day to check if the site worked accurately. This meant that they were able to identify and address any production error quickly and automatically. There were no changes made to the production until the defect was addressed. This was an automated Andon Cord.

Continuous Deployment

Continuous deployment is a scenario that is unimaginable and scary for most startups. The idea of this method is that the startup must update the production systems regularly.

IMVU was regularly updating its production system by running close to fifty updates. This was made possible since they invested in test scripts. Over 14,000 test scripts would run at least 60 times a day and simulate everything from a click on the browser to running the code in the database.

Eric Ries also talks about Wealthfront, which is a company that operates in an environment regulated by the SEC. However, this company practices continuous deployment and has more than ten production releases a day.

Kanban

Kanban is a technique that was borrowed from the world of lean manufacturing. It was developed by Taiichi Ohno in the late 1980s to improve the manufacturing unit of Toyota automobiles. Eric Ries mentions the company Grockit, which is an online tool that helps one build skills for standardized tests. This tool creates a story in the development process, which is then used to develop a feature. They also mention to the user what the outcome or benefit of the tool is. These stories are validated to see how they work for different users. A test is conducted to see how this tool benefits the customer. There are four states:

- Backlog: The tasks that can be worked on but have not yet been started

- In Progress: The tasks that are currently being developed

- Built: The tasks that have been completed and are ready for the customer

- Validated: Products that have been released and have been validated by the customers

If the story fails the validation test, then it will be removed from the product and produced again. A good practice would be to ensure that none of the buckets mentioned above have more than two projects at a given time. If there is a project or task that is in the built bucket, it cannot move to the validated stage until there is enough room for it. The same goes for the processes that are in the backlog bucket. These tasks cannot move to the "In Progress" bucket until it is free.

A valuable outcome of this method is that the team can start measuring its productivity based on the validated learning and feedback from the customer. The team will then stop measuring its productivity based on the number of new features developed.

The Five Whys

Every technical defect or issue has a human cause at its root. The five whys technique will allow the startup to get closer to the root cause. This is a deceptively simple technique but is powerful. Eric Ries has mentioned in his book that most problems or issues that are identified in a process are caused due to a lack of training. These problems may look like an individual's mistake or a technical issue. Ries uses IMVU as an example to explain this technique.

- A new product feature or release was disabled for customers. Why? The feature tanked because of a failed server.

- Why did this server fail? There was a subsystem that was used incorrectly.

- Why was that server used incorrectly? The engineer using the server was not trained to use it properly.

- Why did he not know how to use the server? He was never trained.

- Why was he not trained? His manager did not believe that new engineers needed to be trained since he believed that he and his team were too busy.

This technique is extremely useful for startups since it helps them make improvements within a short period. A huge amount can be invested in training, but this may not be the optimal thing to do when the startup is still at its development stage. If the startup takes a look at the root cause of every problem, it can identify the core areas that need to be worked on and not focus only on the issues at the surface.

Most people tend to overreact to issues that happen at the moment, and the Five Whys help them understand what they need to look at to understand what is happening. There is a possibility that the Five Whys can be used as a way to blame people in the team to see whose fault it was. The goal of this method is to identify problems that are caused not by bad people but by bad processes. Every member of the team must be in the same room when this analysis is made. When blame needs to be taken, the management must take the hit for not having a solution at the system-level. Good practices to follow to get started with this methodology are:

- Mutual empowerment and trust. If a mistake is made for the first time, you should be tolerant of them. Ensure that you do not make the same mistake twice.

- Maintain focus on the system since most mistakes happen due to a flaw in the system and ensure that people always solve problems at the system level.

- The company should always face some unpleasant truths. This method will bring out some unpleasant truths to the surface, and the management should ensure that these issues are taken care of at the initial stage. If this method is not conducted in the right manner, it will change into the Five Blames.

- Always start small and be specific. You have to look at the process in detail and always start with small issues. When you understand the issues, you must identify the solutions. Always run the process regularly and involve as many people from the team as you can.

- Appoint someone who is a master at Five Whys. This person must be the primary change agent and should have a good degree of authority to ensure that things get done. This person will be accountable for judging whether the costs were made to prevent or work on those problems that are paying off or not.

The Five Whys methodology is used to transform the startup into a more organized and adaptive organization, which can be hard.

Chapter Eight: Lean Enterprise

You know what lean is, and you have learned about what a lean startup is. So, what do you think a lean enterprise is? A lean enterprise is an organization that is looking for ways to continuously improve processes. So, it is clear to understand what lean enterprise management is. Lean enterprise management ensures that the organization adheres to the principles of a lean enterprise. In simple words, the manufacturing process should indeed be lean, but the concept of lean should spread across every process in the organization. For instance, the commercial department should always ask itself if there is a better and faster way to give the customer the correct response the first time itself. The purchasing department should ask itself if there is any way they can ensure that the products they purchase are good the first time. Manufacturing is the core of every organization, but the speed of the process is related to every other function in the business. It is for this reason that you can develop a lean enterprise only when you spread the concept of lean across the entire organization.

How to Start to Create a Lean Enterprise

If you want to understand the concept of a lean enterprise better, watch the following video: https://www.whatislean.org/. The concept of a lean enterprise has been explained in detail. Now that you are aware of what a lean enterprise is, you know that all the departments involved in a lean company should also be lean. You may now wonder how human resources or finance departments can be lean. Yes, these departments and every other department in the organization can be lean. They will, however, need to have their own goals, metrics, and board.

The departments should also ensure that they develop metrics that are relevant not only to the customer but also to the company. So, now look at how you can create a lean enterprise. The easiest way to do this is to place a board and write the goal for the department at the center of that board. The only thing you will need to do is follow the steps of lean management and ensure that the department is now lean.

The Difficulties of the Flow of Information

The only reason every organization starts changing the functioning of the manufacturing department is that you can always see what you are trying to improve, and you can see an immediate effect. You will need to be careful when you begin to work with intangible information like:

- Phone

- Mail

- Call

- Chats

- Documents

- Fax, etc.

It is harder to work with intangible information because this information is from multiple channels and at a great speed. You can deal with this intangible information in the following manner:

- Create the standard or the process for the flow of information.

- Draw the process map and include the people involved at every stage of the process.

- Ask the members of the team whether the information is necessary.

You should at least start with the following step: Ask the team who will consume the information that is being collected. You should create the standard or the rules that will define who the supplier of the information is, who the customer is, and what the customer may want or need. You can use the SIPOC tool to perform these steps.

SIPOC to Standardize the Information Flow

Now look at how you can build SIPOC to manage the information flow in your enterprise. Seven steps will help you manage the flow of information:

> 1. You should first identify the process that you wish to map and define the boundary and the scope of that process. You should ensure that you use the right words to describe this process and also assess the time you will take to complete the tasks under each process. Make sure that you list the start and endpoints.

> 2. Make a note of the outputs. You should ensure that you list the products and the services that you will need to produce at the end of the project.

> 3. Ensure that you name the customers, end-users, or the stakeholders by their name and system. You should ensure that you map the correct output to the stakeholder.

> 4. Now, work on determining and defining the requirements.

> 5. Understand what the customers expect from you and what they demand from you. Make sure that you define these based on the budget that you receive.

> 6. Define the inputs you will need for the process. Identify the raw material, the information, capital, human resources,

and natural resources that you will need to use to produce the outputs.

7. Identify the sources of the inputs.

If you want to ensure that you follow a lean process, you will not only have to develop a lean manufacturing environment but will also need to develop a lean enterprise. You should then think broader and work towards changing the point of view of the departments. You can do this by placing a metric board in their offices. This may sound strange, and the people may push back, but you should make an effort. Once you see that there is a change in the way the information flows, you can use SIPOC as the main tool.

Chapter Nine: Lean Teams

The lean project management methodology has changed the way businesses work. This method will help to improve processes for the better. A lean team will enable a company to facilitate a positive change in the way the business manages the process, and will respond to any problems promptly. A lean team is a group of people who can make quick decisions and also take actions that will benefit the company.

Developing a Lean Team

It is important to create an effective lean team. To do this, a business should define the teams around the processes that the teams perform. For these teams to be effective, they will need to include people with diverse backgrounds and capabilities. These people should know how to improve processes.

Forming a Team

Once the project manager or the business has defined the various processes in the business, it is time to develop the team and focus on improving every process. The team should have a set of individuals with diverse capabilities and preferably not from the same department. Look at the example of engineering, procurement, and construction company. This company's current process results in some overpriced bids, which will mean that the company loses the bid. Alternatively, the company could have underpriced bids, which will reduce the revenue of the company.

The current issue can be because of the result of poor communication between the business and the stakeholders during the proposal process. A lean team can improve this communication and also lead to some positive change by including people from the different departments involved in this process. Instead of making any changes based on one team's perspective, if the changes are made based on the input given by different individuals, the changes made to the process will be made based on the input from different departments like:

- The field service team

- Project management

- Purchasing

- Engineering

- Logistics

When you form a lean team with members from different departments working on a specific process, the team can identify the problems and also develop a targeted solution to improve that process.

Empowering the Team

A traditional business structure will result in a vertical power structure where minimal input is received from the employees, which makes it difficult to improve the processes promptly. Lean teams work on addressing this problem by empowering the teams to make the right decisions to facilitate the change. The roles of every team and the responsibilities of every member will be clearly defined. These members can also work on improving processes. The teams must have access to make changes without changing the authority structure.

Lean Team Hierarchy

A lean team also follows a hierarchy similar to the organization hierarchy. This hierarchy will include all the levels of business. There will be a group leader who will facilitate the improvements and communication between the different teams. Each team will have a team leader who is responsible for implementing the changes to the processes and for obtaining feedback from the group leaders. Every team member is responsible for identifying a problem and looking for a solution to that problem. When a potential solution is identified, the team members will work together with the team leader to develop the solution.

One key aspect of a lean team's structure is that every group is empowered to implement some improvements within the scope of the project. If a single improvement impacts multiple groups, the group leader will bring the idea to the upper management for any additional support or approval. This structure will help to ensure that the team can implement a change to the process.

Implementing a Lean Team

If a project manager wants to implement a lean team, they will need to speak to the head of the organization since the implementation will need a top to bottom approach. Every manager, supervisor, employee, or worker must be involved in making the change. A worker or employee should expect the practices to improve, and the management should always support the change. To do this, there must be a fundamental shift in culture. The manager should be trained to lead and facilitate the change, and the team members must learn to improve these processes. It will become slightly difficult to make changes to the workplace culture. It is a good idea to use tools like the Five Whys, Kaizen, or the PDCA (Plan-Do-Check-Act) for this.

Kaizen

Kaizen is a continuous improvement philosophy. If a business wants to use this philosophy, it must ensure that every worker in the firm, right from the CEO to the assistants, is involved in the process. Kaizen will help to change the culture at a workplace by allowing workers to improve processes regularly and allowing the management to support that change.

Five Whys

The five whys will enable the worker to identify the cause of the problem and then fix it. This technique will ensure that they do not focus only on the superficial issues since that will not solve the problems. As the name suggests, the employees should ask "why" until they identify the cause of the problem.

PDCA

PDCA is a lean tool that helps to resolve any issue through four steps: Plan, Do, Check, and Act. When a problem is found, this tool will enable the team member to address it by identifying a solution, testing it, obtaining feedback, and applying it.

How to Build a Lean Team

Eric Ries, in his book *The Startup Way: How Modern Companies Use Entrepreneurial Management to Transform Culture and Drive Long-Term Growth*, describes the mantra of a lean team as "Think big, start small and scale fast." Regardless of whether you are working in a startup or working on building an internal project in an established organization, the lean team approach will maximize the efficiency and the results in uncertain times. That said, it is hard to assemble a group that can execute this vision. This process also comes with the routine challenges and questions that are unique to the methodology. Now, look at seven steps you can use to build a Lean team.

Start Small

Amazon follows the "two-pizza team" approach. In this approach, you must always start with a small team if you want to work on developing new methods. You should aim to develop a team that you can feed easily with just two pizzas. When you have a smaller team, you will see that the members bond faster, which will improve the communication within the team. A small team also ensures that a decision is made quickly, and new methods can be tested faster. There is also better accountability since every member of the team is aware of what they need to do.

Make the Team Cross-Functional

Yes, there are very few people on the team. This does not mean that you do not capitalize on their abilities. Every lean team should be cross-functional, which means that different members of the team should bring out a different ability or skill that will represent the different departments in the company. In enterprise organizations, the teams have employees from the same departments, and once they complete their work, the results or the output will be shared with the next department. This is an inefficient approach since ideas are not shared between departments, which will lead to subpar solutions.

If you want to build a cross-functional team, you should first sit down and understand the needs of the project. You must understand the project and identify the different departments that must be involved to make some progress. You should also identify potential roadblocks and see how they can be avoided. Eric Ries, in his above book, talks about an industrial project. For this project, the team should include a product designer, a member with manufacturing expertise, and marketing or a salesperson who understands the needs of the customers. A project in a different industry will require a different set of people. There are numerous combinations that you can look at, depending on what needs to be achieved at the end of the project.

Every project manager or team leader must be aware of what the project is and also see if they need to obtain some permissions from the legal department. Make sure that you identify the different departments that need to be involved in the project at the start so you can avoid any delays. You can always ask for volunteers if you have issues with finding a person from a specific department to join your team.

Never Over-Rely on Team Players

Most project managers make the mistake of depending on the same employees to ensure that the team works together. This will impact the productivity and satisfaction of those employees since they will be overloaded. A study was conducted by the Harvard Business Review to understand employee satisfaction. The study concluded that employees who are always in high demand because they are seen as collaborators in their company have the lowest career and engagement satisfaction scores. Some experts say that it is easy to prevent overload by reducing some unnecessary meetings, and let individuals know that it is okay for them to say no and let someone else take their place.

Train People to Be Team Smart

It is important to ensure that every employee in a team excels in that team. To do this, you must invest in training. Companies make the mistake of focusing on helping a team member develop professionally at an individual level. They develop training programs that do not focus on teams, but only on people. Managers and employees are never educated on how they can contribute effectively to the team or how to build a better team. Many companies are team dumb since the collective intelligence of the team is independent of the intelligence of the members of the team.

A company with the smartest employees can still have terrible teams. A paper published in 2010 in the *Science* journal showed that the collective intelligence or "c-factor" is correlated with the communication and environment within the team. This factor is dependent on how the conversations take place in the team, the social sensitivity of the group, and the number of women in the group. This research also suggested that teams that fail at completing one task are likely to fail all other tasks as well. You, as the project manager, can increase the c-factor in the team by guiding the different members of the team about how to work together.

Creating a Pro-Risk Environment

If you want to create breakthroughs or find some innovative solutions, you need bold ideas and the willingness to make mistakes. Individuals in lean teams should learn to welcome both failure and risk. It is difficult to create this mindset in teams since most organizations still follow the principle of "failure is not an option". The dynamics of the team will make it hard to change this mindset since every member of the team will want to play it safe. Nobody will ever want to look like a fool in front of their colleagues. That being said, you could use some pragmatic tools and psychological insights to coach your team into feeling brave about failing and taking risks.

Each member of the team has a different trait, but since everyone is a human being, most of their behavioral and psychological patterns are the same. This may seem obvious to you now, but the truth is that people often overlook this insight. Companies only focus on the personalities, capabilities, and expertise of the individuals they hire, but research states that people with different capabilities can work together and deliver projects on time if the right environment is created for them.

It is important to let your teams know that their decisions will not result in litigation or a loss of millions of dollars. You must help your teams understand what can be undone and what cannot. A team should have a reverse button at some point where they can step back, accept that it is not going to work, and try a different approach. They should, however, make those decisions quickly. If the team works on identifying the reversible risks, people will not be bogged down because this will reduce the chance of a blame game.

Understanding the Needs of the Team

Every member of a team will join that team with specific assumptions in mind, and they work on trying to understand how to get their work done. They also have some assumptions about how the communication in the team should work. If you want to ensure that your team works as a cohesive unit, you must understand the different assumptions that each individual is working with. Every team member walks around the team with an assumption about how each member of the team should behave. If there is an individual who constantly interrupts people, the other members of the team may believe that he or she is a jerk.

It is for this reason that experts recommend that every team should develop a charter of norms. These norms will answer simple questions like:

- How do we want to work together?

- How do we react to a situation where we disagree with each other?

- Are we going to make some proposals?

- Are there going to be arguments about tasks?

- How do we come to a decision?

When you develop the charter, identify the different scales that you want to cover. Ensure that you cover the scales surrounding evaluating, scheduling, communicating, disagreeing, trusting, persuading, deciding, and leading.

Measure to Learn and Improve the Team

Regardless of whether you want to build a new team or improve an existing team, you cannot simply start without considering the team and measuring the team. Your measurements do not have to be elaborate, and they can be as simple as assessing the current sentiment in the team. By this, you should try to understand how people feel about the team spirit. You can assess this during every team meeting. Ask your team members to give the team a rating between one and five. If they are not comfortable about sharing the rating in front of the entire team, you can ask them to rate the team on a piece of paper. When you receive the information, you must act on that information. For instance, if most members of the team have rated the spirit as one, you should spend some time to understand why they feel this way and work towards developing a solution to cater to the problem. When you do this, you apply the build-measure-learn lean startup methodology to your team.

Teams do vary across a company, but a lean team will only be effective if it is small, and the members have diverse capabilities. It is important for you, as the project manager, to create ground rules, ensure that every member contributes, and check in with the team to assess how individuals feel about the team and the environment. From here, you can work on the feedback you receive and improve the processes. You must remember that you and your team should work towards continuous improvement, and this means that you can never accept that your team is perfect.

Chapter Ten: What Is Lean Analytics?

Lean Analytics is an innovative and great method to help you streamline the sales funnel. When you combine this method with the psychological insight of American author Nir Eyal's, you can guarantee success. From the previous chapter, you will have understood what the Lean Startup approach is and the different techniques and tools you can use to follow this approach. Lean Analytics is only an extension of the lean startup method. Alistair Croll and Benjamin Yoskovitz, in their book *Lean Analytics: Use Data to Build a Better Startup Faster*, wrote that a lean startup would help you structure the progress and also help you identify the risky parts of the business. The lean startup method will also help you learn more about how you can adapt and overcome these risks. Lean Analytics is used to measure the team's progress and also help the business answer some questions to get the required answers.

What Kind of Business Are You?

Lean Analytics is one of the best ways to streamline sales funnel. The idea behind this approach is that when you know the type of business you are in and also the stage your business is at, you can track the important metrics and optimize those metrics. These metrics will be the ones that matter most to your business.

Croll and Yoskovitz described the five stages that every startup will go through if it wants to implement lean analytics:

Empathy

In this stage, the business should work towards understanding the customers better. The business should learn more about the problems that they want to solve and work towards building a project that will solve these problems.

Stickiness

When it comes to stickiness, the business should look at how it can develop a product to engage the customer.

Virality

In this stage, the business should focus on user acquisition. In simple words, the business should try to identify the onboarding process.

Revenue

The business will now need to focus on monetizing the product.

Scale

It is finally time for you to expand your sales and diversify.

How to Apply Lean Analytics

Lean analytics, like every other approach, has its canvas. This is an across-the-board tool, and you can use this tool for different methods or processes. A Scrum expert, Nicolas Nemmi, developed the lean roadmap canvas based on the hooked model developed by Nir Eyal.

The Lean Roadmap

	Hook Model			
	Trigger	Action	Variable Reward	Investment
Empathy				
Stickness				
Virality				
Revenue				
Scale				

Lean Analytics Stage

By Nicolas Nemni (@nicolasegosum). Based on the theories of Nir Eyal (@nireyal), Alistair Croll (@acroll) & Ben Yoskovitz (@byosko)

There are four boxes in the canvas developed by Nemmi, and each of these boxes is combined with the five lean analytics stages described above.

Trigger

The trigger will define what it will take to ensure that the user gets to the product.

Action

This will help you define the simplest behavior in anticipation of the reward or feedback. In other words, you are looking for a way to make it easier to remove any friction in the buying process. An example of this is Amazon's 1-Click ordering. This method accomplishes the goal.

Variable Reward

This will help you define if the reward is fulfilling, but leaves the user wanting some more. Candy manufacturers are brilliant at doing this.

Investment

What is the customer doing to ensure that he or she returns to purchase your products? If the customer is looking for a way to increase their reach through social media, you should see how the customer can achieve this.

How to Use the Lean Analytics Canvas

It is a good idea to use a lean analytics canvas when you want to understand or view some data. Look at how you can use this canvas:

- Choose the required result or the outcome for the project

- Choose the dates against which you can meet a goal or an objective, and set the goal against that date

- Make the list of functionalities and actions that you will need to complete to achieve this goal

- Test the functionality one at a time and implement that functionality

- Measure the impact of the functionality on the process

- Proceed to the next box once you meet the desired goal

PART THREE: Agile Project Management

Chapter Eleven: What Is The Agile Framework?

The Agile framework, unlike other project management methodologies or frameworks, focuses on iterating quickly and satisfying the demands of customers. The Agile framework is based on the Agile Manifesto, which will be looked at later in this chapter. The agile framework can either be called a methodology or a process. One of the values in the Agile manifesto states that the philosophy prioritizes interactions and individuals over tools and processes. Most agile teams use these frameworks as the starting point, and they customize the elements in the methodology to meet their needs.

Organizations use different agile frameworks, and most of them modify some parts of the framework as per their needs and build their agile processes. Now look at some of the common agile frameworks in the industry:

- Scrum

- Adaptive Software Development (ASD)

- Extreme Programming (XP)
- Scaled Agile Framework (SAFe)
- The Crystal Method
- Rapid Application Development (RAD)
- Dynamic Systems Development Method (DDSM)
- Disciplined Agile (DA)
- Lean Software Development (LSD)
- Feature Driven Development (FDD)

Which Framework is Best?

Since there are numerous agile processes in the market, it is hard to choose the right one. That being said, there is no CORRECT agile process that you can choose from. You must consider different factors about your business before you choose the framework that will work best for you. Some of these factors include:

- Structure/size of your product portfolio
- Company size
- Needs of stakeholders
- Available resources
- Team structure

Every framework has its pros and cons, and a framework that works for one business does not necessarily work for your business. You should experiment and try the frameworks before you identify the framework that works best for you.

Scrum, Extreme Programming and Kanban

Now look at some of the common agile frameworks in the industry: Scrum and Kanban. Scrum is an agile framework that gives an organization the capability to manage and control incremental and iterative projects of different types. Two other agile frameworks that are accepted by the industry are Kanban and Extreme Programming.

The core principles of extreme programming are engineering principles. Organizations following this approach focus primarily on the delivery of high-quality software. A team using this framework or methodology collaborates and works in short, flexible development cycles, and they are eager to adapt and change the methods used in the development of the output. In Extreme programming, teams work on small user stories and plan small releases or prototypes of the output to obtain feedback from the clients or stakeholders.

Kanban is another agile methodology that focuses on the visualized workflow. In this method, the work is broken down into smaller sections or pieces that can easily be managed by the team. The Kanban methodology helps organizations and project managers identify the waste or bottlenecks in their processes. It also helps teams reduce the wait time between the work done and the delivery of the product. Kanban can do this since the methodology adheres to strict process policies and helps the teams manage and measure the flow of work.

The Agile Manifesto

Scrum is a framework and not a mathematical process or methodology. You still need to think and make choices. One of the biggest advantages of the Scrum framework is that you can make discretionary decisions that are best for you, based on the feedback you receive from your customers.

In 2001, seventeen software and project experts, who were successful in their divergent processes, agreed upon the following values that best suited their programming methodologies.

They believed that they uncovered better ways of developing software and wanted to help people all over the world do it better, too. These values formed the Agile Manifesto, and any project management tool that uses agile must adhere to these values:

- Interactions and individuals take precedence over tools and processes

- Working software is more important than comprehensive documentation

- Collaborate with customers before you begin any negotiations

- Always respond to change and tweak your plans whenever necessary

This means that the team should be concerned more about the items on the left in the points mentioned above.

Even though the Agile Manifesto and principles were written by and for software experts, the values remain valid for any Scrum project you embark upon. Just like GPS was designed by and for the military, it does not mean that people cannot benefit from it when they sit in their car and head towards a new part of town. For more information on the history of the agile manifesto and its founders, visit http://agilemanifesto.org.

Agile Principles

The founders of Agile did not stop only at the values. They also defined twelve principles to expand on those values. You can use these values in your Scrum project to check if your framework adheres to the goals of agile:

- It is important to satisfy the customer by delivering the product or software early. The alternative approach is to deliver smaller sections of the product to the customers.

- Ask your customers for feedback and make changes to the product, even if it is late in the development stage. Every agile process allows you to make some changes to the product to improve customer satisfaction.

- Deliver working prototypes of the software at regular intervals to the customer.

- Developers and business people should work together throughout the project.

- You should give the developing team all the support it needs to ensure that the job is done.

- Have regular meetings where you can convey information to the team effectively and efficiently.

- You can measure your progress by preparing working prototypes of the software.

- Developers, sponsors, and users should maintain a constant pace throughout the project.

- Good design and attention to technical detail enhance agility.

- It is essential to keep the process simple. This means that you should maximize the amount of work your team does not have to do.

- Self-organizing teams provide the best designs and architecture.

- The team should reflect on what it should do better to become more effective and then adjust its behavior accordingly.

The principles do not change, but the tools and techniques to achieve them can.

Some of the principles will be easier to implement than others. Consider, for example, principle two. Maybe your company (or group or family) is open to change and new ideas. To them, Scrum is natural, and they are ready to get started. But on the other hand, some may be more resistant to change.

How about principle six? Is working face to face possible in your project? With the Internet and globalization of workforces, you may have team members from India to Russia to the United States of America. Instead of worrying about how this principle cannot apply to your team, you should identify a solution. Can you use Hangouts or Skype to stay in touch with your team? Do you prefer a teleconference? This is not the intention of the sixth principle, but if you are to improve tomorrow, you should focus on how to deal with today. This means that you should learn to adapt to change.

You are bound to have unique challenges. Do not let a hiccup or less-than-perfect scenario stop your team from working on the project. Part of the fun in using Scrum is to work through issues and get to the results. The same goes for the twelve principles. If you adhere to the principles listed above, you can improve your team's efficiency and quality.

Platinum Principles

Experts will suggest that you use these principles when you work on a project since they improve efficiency and assist in the implementation of the process.

Visualize Instead of Writing

Overall, people are visual. They think pictorially and remember pictorially. For those old enough to remember encyclopedias, which part did you like best? Most kids like pictures and adults are no different. They are still more likely to read a magazine flipping first through images, and then sometimes going back for articles that piqued their interest (if at all).

Pictures, diagrams, and graphs instantly relay information. However, if you write out a report, people will stop reading if there are no diagrams to support the claims made in the report.

Twitter was interested in studying the effectiveness of tweets with photos versus those that were text only. It conducted a study using SHIFT Media Manager and came up with some interesting results. Users engaged five times more frequently when tweets included photos as opposed to text-only tweets. The rate of retweets and replies with photos doubled. However, the cost per engagement of photo tweets was half that of text-only tweets.

When possible, encourage your team to present information visually, even if that means sketching a diagram on a whiteboard. If anybody does not understand it, they can ask, and changes can be made immediately. Also, with technology today, you can make simple graphs, charts, and models easily.

Think and Act as a Team

The heart of Scrum is working as a team; however, the team environment can, at first, be unsettling because, in the US corporate culture, the opposite is encouraged—an individual competes with his or her peers. "How well can I succeed in this environment so that I stand out and get the next promotion?"

In Scrum, the project survives or dies at the team level. By leveraging the individual's talent to that of a team, you take the road from average to hyper-productive. According to Aristotle, "The whole is greater than the sum of its parts."

How do you create this team culture? The Scrum framework itself emphasizes the team. Physical space, common goals, and collective ownership all scream team. Then add the following to your Scrum frame:

- Eliminate work titles. No one "owns" areas of development. Skills and contribution establish status.

- Pair team members to enhance cross-functionality and front-load quality assurance, then switch the pairings often.

- Always report with team metrics, not an individual or pairing metrics.

Avoiding Formality

Have you ever seen a knockout PowerPoint presentation and wondered how much time someone spent putting it together?

You should never think about doing this for a Scrum project since you will be wasting too much time. Instead, you can scribble it on a flip chart in 1/1000th of the time and stick it up on a wall where people will look at it and then get back to creating value. If it requires discussion, walk over to the concerned parties and ask them now or whenever the need arises. Focus your valuable time and effort on the product instead of prepared presentations.

Atos Origin produced independent research showing that the average corporate employee spends close to 40 percent of his or her working day on internal emails that do not add any value to the business. This means that the real workweek does not start until Wednesday.

Pageantry is too often mistaken for professionalism and progress. In Scrum projects, you are encouraged to communicate immediately, directly, and informally whenever you have a question. You also save time since you work closely with the other members of the team. You should identify the simplest way you can get what you need with the goal of delivering the highest-quality product in mind.

Before long, your projects will evolve a Scrum culture. As people become educated on the process and see the improved results, their buy-in for barely enough will increase accordingly. So, bear through any initial push back with education, patience, and consistency.

Chapter Twelve: Start An Agile Project

Most traditional project management methodologies use a linear process. Here, you will understand the project, plan the tasks, decide on a strategy, and build the right solution to cater to the problem before you move it to production. You will then fix any problems in that solution using data from regular assessments. This is also known as the waterfall approach since it includes cascading steps. Traditional project management methods do have issues with the timeline and budget since conventional development sequences do not allow for any changes in the requirement. These sequences do not allow the teams to make any changes to the demands of the clients or budget.

Understanding Agile Project Management

In the previous chapter, you learned more about what the agile framework is. You know that the agile framework does not focus on fixed sequences, but works in cycles that facilitate continuous collaboration, improvement, and innovation. The customer or client is always involved in the project. Now look at what agile project management is all about.

Understand the Problem

It is important to understand what your customers or clients need. To do this, you should ask them about the different problems that they are facing, and what the problem statement is. As an agile project manager, it is important to focus on the end-user. You may need to conduct thorough research of the market or conduct interviews with the customers to answer these questions. In simple words, you should focus on trying to understand how to measure your success.

Assemble the Right Team

Now that you have understood the problem, you should focus on trying to set up a team that has the necessary experience and skills to solve the problem. This may mean that you need to bring in people from different departments or hire external consultants. In some situations, you will also need to develop the skills of the existing team members.

Brainstorm

The team can now work on developing ideas on how to solve the problem. At this point, every idea should be looked at. Ensure that you encourage every member of the team to innovate.

Build an Initial Prototype

Once you have identified the potential solution, you should work on developing a prototype. This will not take too much time, and you should remember that agile is a project management methodology based on creativity and flexibility. Once you build the prototype, let the customers look at the prototype so they can give you their opinion or feedback. If the feedback is negative, inform the team that they will need to work on a different model which aligns to the customers' requirement. This is one of the best approaches since you learn the issues with the design very early, which gives you sufficient time to make the required changes. You will not risk working for days or months on a prototype, and realize at the end of the project that this is not a good fit for your client.

Decide the Boundaries

Based on the feedback you receive from the clients, you should decide the scope of the project. You can add or remove features based on the feedback you receive for the prototype. You can maintain a document that outlines the scope of the project, and update that document whenever necessary. You should also update that document as the project progresses.

Plan the Major Milestones Using A Roadmap

The next step is to set the milestones that you and your team must meet when developing the product. You do not have to add too many details to this roadmap. In fact, it is important that the milestones you set are easy to meet and flexible. You can, however, decide the different components that you will use to make that product and ensure that you meet the deadlines.

It is not only the features of the product that you should look at, but you should also look at the goals. For example, if your client wants to build on their customer base, you should understand how they plan to achieve that goal. Ensure that you know exactly what needs to be done to meet your customers' demands.

Plan Sprints

Sprints are short development cycles that last anywhere between one and four weeks. If you want to ensure that the development rate is stable, you should maintain the same length for every sprint. When you plan a sprint, you should devise the list of tasks that the team should complete and choose realistic targets.

The goal is to assemble a product that is functional in the shortest time frame. Your team can then work on improving that product in the subsequent sprints. You can ensure that the product is developed successfully only when every member of the team collaborates and cooperates. People in the team should always be given a chance to express their concerns or opinions.

Check In Every Day

A daily stand-up or meeting will make it easier for you to identify any issues early in the project. A stand-up is a small meeting, around fifteen minutes long, where all the members of the team will talk about their progress. Every team member should tell you what he or she worked on for the previous day, what they want to achieve today, and whether there are any concerns or problems that they have identified. It is your responsibility as the project manager to keep the team on track and ensure that you work with them to resolve any issues.

Review the Sprint

You should sit down with your team when the sprint ends and evaluate the progress of the team. Ask them what they thought they did well, the lessons they learned, the parts of the task that they can improve, etc. It is important to review and have meetings with your team daily to monitor the health of the project.

You should also ask your team to give you real-time project updates and ensure that you always keep the clients in the loop. Your clients should also be given the freedom to check up on the project at any time and give you feedback. The client should be made aware that the team is working on the project. When you interact with your clients regularly, you can iron out any bugs.

Plan the Next Sprint

You should always use the sprint system until you complete your project. Ensure that you are open to change and always make changes to the process based on the end-user or client feedback. You must always strive for excellence and never forget about the design. If you follow the agile project management methodology, you need to rely on both technical expertise and strong interpersonal connections. You must choose an effective communication channel and ensure that the entire team uses it.

Completion and Release

Once you develop the product, and you receive positive feedback from the end-users and clients, you can manufacture that product and release it into the market. The agile project approach, however, does not end here. You will need to make some adjustments to the product if there are any defects or bugs in it.

You will learn to communicate better with every project. It may be hard to cope with agile project management, at first, but you will soon begin to wonder why you ever used traditional project management methods.

Chapter Thirteen: Agile Versus Scrum Versus Kanban

Over the years, project management has significantly evolved, and numerous project management tools help to make those changes to project management. If there is someone following a project management trend, they will know that technology is only a small part of that discussion. Agile, Kanban and Scrum, and other project management methodologies dominate the discussion. In this chapter, you will understand these terms and look at the difference between these methods.

Differences Between Agile, Kanban and Scrum

Agile is a project management methodology used to break the tasks in a complex project into smaller chunks of work that can be managed easily. Agile project management was earlier used in software development projects to improve the speed at which the project is completed, but it is now being used in different industries. Agile is a set of principles that were defined in the Agile manifesto, and these have been defined in the previous chapters. Kanban and Scrum are two methodologies that follow Agile principles. In simple words, if you want to implement an agile framework in your business, you can use Scrum or Kanban to do this. This definition was proposed by Nicholas Carrier, Associate Partner at London-based Prophet.

Kanban and Scrum are agile project management methodologies that have some differences. Carrier noted that these methods also have some similarities. Each of these methods uses a board that shows the project manager the status of the tasks where people will move between the three categories:

1. Tasks that have not been started
2. Tasks that are in progress
3. Tasks that are complete

Differences Between Scrum and Kanban

Both Scrum and Kanban share some similar traits, and people make the incorrect assumption that both Scrum and Kanban are two sides of the same coin. This is far from the truth since these agile methodologies are very different. The Scrum methodology will break the development cycle time into work periods with time limits called sprints. These sprints last for a maximum of two weeks. Jessica D'Amato, who is a project manager at Dragon Army, said that a project manager could plan the initiatives that should be completed by the team within a two-week sprint. They should also hold meetings to understand the progress and how the task is moving along. A project manager also uses this meeting to demo any new releases to the client before they launch it. There are three prescribed roles in Scrum:

Product Owner

The product owner focuses on the initial planning of the tasks. He or she also works on prioritizing the task and communicating with every member of the team.

Scrum Master

The Scrum Master is responsible for assessing the status of every process during a two-week sprint.

Team Members

A team member is an individual who will carry the tasks out in a two-week sprint.

Scrum follows a pre-defined structure or framework while Kanban does not. Kanban is a methodology based only on the list of items or tasks that are in the backlog. There is no set time within which a task on the Kanban board needs to be completed, but every task on the board is given a priority. This board has different columns, which make it easier for the project manager to know the status of any task in the project. They will know which task is currently being worked on and which task is completed.

Joe Garner, who is the project manager in a computer design firm, mentioned that Kanban focuses on improving every aspect of the process. Kanban is a method that can be used to manage the creation of any product with the vision of delivering the output. This project management methodology can enhance the processes being followed in a company by improving them without making a change to the entire system.

Agile Pros and Cons

Garner talks about how agile methodologies like Kanban and Scrum can provide an iterative and incremental approach to complete any project when compared to traditional project management methods where a linear approach is followed. He mentioned that Agile focuses on the different business requirements and also creates the product, which will need to be delivered to the customer. This product is released in small units. The Agile framework focuses on accountability, transparency, and strong teamwork. This will ensure that the product aligns with the goals of the company and the client.

As Garner mentioned, agile management gives the teams the flexibility to improve their processes continuously. Having said that, this could lead to some delay in the final delivery date. This problem often arises in a digital transformation team since the executives believe the agile methodology, but they do not have the necessary resources to work iteratively on a process and improve it. When this happens, a team may be under too much stress to complete work on time. They will then switch to the old methods, which will result in the delivery of a product with low quality.

Scrum Pros and Cons

The Delivery Manager at Oak Brook, Brijmohan Bhavsar, talks about how Scrum provides high visibility and transparency of the projects. It also allows the team to accommodate changes to the tasks or processes with ease. In addition to this, Garner also mentioned that Scrum helps to define the roles of every team member. It also enables better collaboration, which will ensure that a project is completed faster. Carrier mentioned that they use Scrum in strategy projects as well since this enables them to communicate with business stakeholders from different departments like technology, marketing, and operations frequently. It allows the teams to collaborate and make the right decisions to obtain the required outcome. Bhavsar also mentioned that breaking a complex task into smaller chunks of work could lead to creating a poorly defined task that could affect the scope of the project.

Kanban Pros and Cons

Kanban is a model used to present any change using additional improvements. This methodology gives a visual of what the team is currently doing. The Kanban board plays an important role in displaying the tasks and workflow. Bhavsar believes that the board also assists with optimizing the tasks that each team must perform. Carrier, however, mentioned that the Kanban methodology could lead to poor productivity since it lacks a structured framework. Kanban does not focus on a cross-functional team since it does not use sprints. He believes that a sprint will help to assign the time a team can take to perform the task. A sprint will drive the team to work towards delivering the process at an increased speed. This is important for digital transformation.

Which One Should You Choose?

You should look at the business requirements before you make the decision between which agile methodology to implement or whether you should implement the agile framework in your business. Bhavsar states that it is best to make this decision based on whether you want the project to be completed faster or if you want to improve the process. He mentioned that it is a good idea to use Scrum if you only want to work on producing work faster. If you want to improve your processes, you should use Kanban. If you want to use a linear workflow, you should implement a waterfall model.

Chapter Fourteen: Step-By-Step Scrum

Scrum is a project management tool that allows teams to use their experiences to make decisions about the project. This tool is a great way for teams to organize their projects, regardless of their size. Through Scrum, a team can identify if the process or approach it plans to use to meet the objective or vision will generate the intended results.

If there is a task that you need to complete, you can use Scrum to provide some structure to your approach. This will help to increase efficiency and improve results. Scrum breaks the tasks down into manageable pieces and prioritizes those tasks depending on what the customer demands. This will help you identify the tasks that you need to complete today, tomorrow, and the next day. You can also see how well you are progressing and where you should adjust to counter any inefficiencies in your approach. This will help you improve your speed and efficiency.

Arts used the concept of empirical exposure modeling since the beginning of time. For example, a sculptor will use a chisel on the material he or she is using to make a sculpture and will check the results before he makes any adaptations. We now use this concept to work on developing software. In this method, the developer does not use a simulation to understand how the project will progress. Instead, he observes actual results and learns from those experiences to develop the project.

Basics of Scrum

A scrum is a tool that helps you devise a process that you can use to develop or manage a task. It provides a framework that will allow you to define the roles of every team member and the work that each member must complete. You can use this framework to prioritize your work and become more efficient in completing the assigned task. Frameworks are not as prescriptive as methodologies since they allow you to add structures, tools, and processes that will complement the primary task. Through this approach, you can observe the process and include other processes that work well with the basic processes wherever necessary to enhance the process. You can complete a task in a few hours or weeks using this framework.

Using Scrum, you can improve the performance of your team at a nascent stage since this project management methodology uses a gradual and repetitive method. When you use the Scrum project management methodology, you should let your team members choose the tools that they can use to improve their performance or conclude the process. There will be no hierarchy in the management, which will reduce the number of progress reports and redundant meetings. If the objective is to get the job done, you should use Scrum since it will help you improve your process.

Scrum is a term used in rugby. The teams form a Scrum or huddle where the forwards from one team interlock their arms and push against the forwards of the opposing team who also have their arms interlocked. The referee then throws the ball into the middle of this huddle. The players work as a team to move the ball down the field. Scrum is like rugby in the sense that it relies on people from different domains with different responsibilities to work towards a common goal.

People believe that only processes in IT, software development, or other technical processes can use Scrum. What they are unaware of is that you can use Scrum to improve any process regardless of whether it is small, large, personal, social, or artistic.

The Roadmap to Value

There are some techniques that you can apply as an extension to Scrum. It is important to remember that these extensions cannot replace Scrum but only improve its function. This book only recommends the practices that experts across the globe have tried and tested. You can decide if you want to use these extensions to improve Scrum, depending on your project.

The aggregation of the common practices of Scrum is known as the roadmap to value. This map consists of seven stages that help you define the vision of your project all the way through the process. In other words, these stages will help you understand what you want to achieve at every stage of the cycle.

Once you define the vision, you can break it into smaller segments to see how you can achieve it. You can then develop a cycle that is efficient and provides results every day, week, and month. The stages are as follows:

- Vision

- Product Roadmap

- Release Planning

- Sprint Planning

- Daily Scrum

- Sprint Review

- Sprint Retrospective

If there is an idea lurking at the back of your mind for years, you can finally put it into action using these seven stages. You will learn more about these stages throughout the book. These stages give you information about the feasibility of your project. You will also learn which parts of the process need improvement.

A Simple Overview

Scrum is a circular and simple process that allows you to inspect and adapt to changes in the process constantly. This section provides an overview of the Scrum process.

Product Backlog

Scrum breaks the process into smaller pieces of work and creates a to-do list for the team. This list is known as the product backlog, and you should follow this list to ensure that your process is efficient and flawless.

Prioritize

Scrum then labels the tasks on the list based on priority. The team should ensure that it completes tasks with a high-priority within a specific period. This period is known as a sprint, and it defines the amount of time a member should spend on the task.

Scrum allows you to quickly adapt to technology, constraints, new innovations, regulations, and market forces. The objective is to work on tasks with high priority and complete them within the prescribed time. All high-priority items go through the following steps:

- Defining the requirement
- Designing
- Developing the requirement
- Testing the process
- Integrating feedback into the process
- Documenting the process

- Confirmation of approval from the stakeholders

Every task on the list will go through the steps mentioned above, regardless of how big or small the task is.

When Scrum decides that a process or task is shippable, you can release it to the customers and take their feedback. You do not have to worry about whether the end-users will like the product or not. Instead, you can work on high-priority tasks and show the stakeholders some tangible results. You can also ask them for feedback and use that feedback to improve the process or generate a new task. During the Scrum meetings, the development team and product owner will add these tasks to the product backlog. You can then prioritize these tasks against the existing ones in the product backlog.

As a process developer, you know that effectiveness is more important when compared to efficiency. You will learn to be efficient if you have an effective team or process. As a team, you should focus on high-priority tasks first. Management consultant, educator, and author, Peter F. Drucker rightly said, "There is nothing as useless as doing efficiently that which should not be done at all."

When the team completes a task, it can share the results with the stakeholders. There are times when the stakeholders will give you some feedback about the process. You should learn to incorporate that feedback into the process and work on the requirement again. Ultimately, you will develop a process that is effective. You will also learn to deliver the results faster and with better quality.

Teams

Regardless of the scope of your project, your team will have similar characteristics. The size of the team will vary, but the roles of the members of the team will remain the same. This book will cover the roles of each member in detail.

The heart of every team is the development team, and these members work together to develop the product. The development team works closely with the Scrum master and the product owner. The roles of both the Scrum master and product owner will be detailed, but in simple words, their roles align the development process to the needs of the stakeholders. They also help to eliminate any distractions for the development team, which allows the team to focus only on their job—developing! The Scrum team is accountable for every task in the cycle. As a team, the members should identify the most effective way to achieve their objectives regardless of the environment they are in.

Stakeholders are not a part of the Scrum team, but it is important to include them since their feedback will impact your project. These stakeholders can be internal or external and include customers, the marketing team, investors, and the legal team.

Governance

The product owner, development team, and scrum master are the three independent units of a scrum team. These units should work together to improve the efficiency of the processes and the team.

Product Owner

The scrum cycle defines the different requirements that the team has to meet or develop. It does not look at the amount of work that the team needs to complete at the end of every sprint. For instance, if the team is working towards developing software, the objective that the team may have set is to develop a prototype at the end of the sprint where the user can easily be moved from the landing page onto the main website. The product owner will need to speak to the stakeholders to understand what the requirements are and prioritize those requirements. They will then need to pass this information on to the development team.

Development Team

The development team will always look at the features that the product manager has listed after having a discussion with the stakeholder. The team can then decide the tasks that they can address or complete in a sprint.

Scrum Master

The scrum master can choose the different processes the team must follow to develop the final product.

The developers of Scrum did not simply assign these roles, but they used their project management experience to establish these roles and define them. The developers are aware of different types of teams and know what works best for the team. It is important to ensure that Scrum teams only have full-time resources. When you share resources between processes, they will tire out and will stop working to their full potential. Have you ever heard of a football team having part-time players? If there is such a team, it will not be a successful one.

Scrum Framework

As mentioned earlier, Scrum is not just a methodology but also a framework. This framework allows every member of the team to understand their responsibilities. It also gives the team a chance to inspect the different elements in the cycle and include some new elements to the process if required. They can also include new processes to the product backlog based on feedback. This framework also provides some processes and tools that teams can use to meet their timelines.

Scrum follows a 3-3-5 framework.

- Three artifacts

- Three roles

- Five events

These elements fit into the cycle. Since the scrum framework follows an iterative and incremental cycle, you can learn new ways to improve that process using the Scrum cycle. The scrum framework is quite straightforward.

Artifacts

- Sprint Backlog

- Product Backlog

- Product Increment

Roles

- Development Team

- Product Owner

- Scrum Master

Events

- Daily Scrum

- Sprint

- Sprint Planning

- Sprint Review

- Sprint Retrospective

The artifacts in the above list are related to the work or tasks that the teams should finish. These artifacts also include the requirements or the demands of the end-users or customers, which can be completed in one scrum cycle. It is important for the team to review the artifacts during the scrum cycle and ensure that the team is working towards completing or meeting the objective.

Every artifact, event, and role have an important purpose in the scrum. Use the roadmap mentioned above to complete any task or project. It is important to remember that Scrum is merely a framework that helps you see what you are doing and where you are in the process. You can choose from the different techniques or tools that you think are necessary to complete any project. Scrum does not define the processes that a team should follow to meet the objective.

One can understand scrum easily, but it is slightly difficult to implement. How to set up a scrum team will be detailed later in this chapter.

Feedback

Scrum, unlike other project management methodologies, allows the team to obtain feedback from the end-users or stakeholders whenever the team completes a task in the backlog. The team will, therefore, learn more about the processes and see which ones are working for them and which need improvement. The teams can also identify the areas where they should enhance efficiency.

The feedback loop works in the following manner:

- The feedback is shared daily between the members of the teams since they work on different tasks in the sprint

- The product owner and the development share feedback every day

- The feedback from the product owner when the end-user accepts or rejects any requirement

- When the sprint is complete, the team will receive some feedback from the business

- The marketplace will provide some feedback to the development team when the product is released into the market

A team can learn more about the processes if it follows the scrum methodology when compared to the traditional project management methods. The latter focuses only on the development of the artifact, while the former only focuses on continuous development. Since you receive regular feedback from the stakeholders about the requirement, you will know what changes to make to the process at an early stage to ensure that you release the final product into the market. At the end of the project, the team does not have to worry about how the customers or end-users perceive their products because you have been communicating and receiving feedback from them all along the way.

Steps to Follow

Here are some steps that you can use to implement Scrum at your workplace.

Define the Scrum Team

A scrum team usually has a minimum of five members and a maximum of eight. These members have a combination of capabilities and can include people from different departments. The members of the team will work together. This team is responsible for delivering the product requirements at the end of every sprint.

Define the Sprint Length

The sprint is a time-box, which can last anywhere between seven and 30 days, and the length of the sprint will remain the same across the entire project. The team will have a planning meeting before every sprint. It is during this meeting that the work for the sprint is planned, and the team will commit to completing this work by the end of the sprint. At the end of the sprint, a meeting is held to review the work completed during the sprint. It is during this meeting that the improvements are reviewed, and the next sprint is planned. If you do not know how long the sprint should be, you can start with a minimum of two weeks.

Appoint the Scrum Master

The Scrum master is the most important person of the scrum team. A scrum master should ensure that the group is effective and progresses well. In the event that there is an issue in the project, the scrum master will work on resolving that issue for the team. The Scrum master is the project manager for the scrum team, except that he or she cannot decide what task the team can work on. This person should avoid micro-managing the team. The scrum master will help the team plan the workflow for the project.

Appoint the Product Owner

A product owner is a person who will be in charge of the team, and he or she must ensure that the team always produces some value to the business, stakeholder, client, or the end-user. The product owner will write the requirements of the clients in the form of a story and will prioritize that story and add it to the product backlog.

Create the Initial Backlog

The product backlog contains a wish list of the requirements or user stories, and it is expected that you complete these tasks in the project. An important story or requirement should always be present at the top of the backlog list. The list of tasks in the backlog should always be ranked based on their importance. A backlog will contain two types of items:

Epics

A high-level story or requirement has a very rough sketch. There are very few details about the story.

Stories

A story is a more detailed requirement that includes the different tasks that should be completed. You can break an epic into numerous stories. You can also break a story down into smaller tasks that a team can work on. Every story can be a different type, including defect/bug, development, chore, etc. Any member of the team can write a new story and add that to the product backlog at any time.

When you go further into the backlog and look at the items at the bottom of the list, these requirements will be epics because they do not have too much detail. An epic or story will rise in priority, depending on the details it contains. These details make it easier for the teams to work on the tasks. A product owner can re-prioritize the backlog as they see fit and at any time during the project.

Plan the Start of The First Sprint

Based on how the team prioritizes the tasks in the backlog, the members can pick the items on that list. The usual process followed is to choose the task with the highest priority. The team should then brainstorm and decide on how much of the task in the backlog they can complete before the next sprint. When the team agrees on the decision made, the sprint will start. The team should now work on developing the stories.

Close the Current Sprint and Start the Next One

When the team finishes a sprint, it is important to ensure that the team completes all the work planned for the sprint. If this is not the case, the team should decide if the work that is left is moved to the next sprint or whether it should move to the backlog.

The team will now review and discuss what processes worked well during the sprint and also identify the processes that should be improved in the next sprint. The team should then discuss and plan the next sprint. This process is repeated until the final sprint is completed. There is no limit on the number of sprints that a team can have in a project, except if there is a strict deadline or if the entire backlog is complete. If these criteria are not met, the sprint will continue indefinitely.

Chapter Fifteen: Create A Kanban Project

As mentioned earlier, businesses use the Kanban methodology to manage processes or workflows while the tasks are in progress. To do this, businesses use Kanban boards that are present in the management system. A Kanban board can be used to visualize the workflow and understand the stage of every task in the workflow. The objective of this system is to identify the potential bottlenecks or impediments in the tasks and identify a solution or fix the issue.

A Brief History

Kanban was developed by the Japanese Industrial Engineer and Businessman for Toyota automotive, Taiichi Ohno, in the 1940s. He created the Kanban system to help the various teams involved in the manufacture of a car to plan their work. It also helped these teams identify any potential issues and develop a solution for those issues. The Kanban software aimed to manage the workflow at every stage of the process.

Taiichi Ohno developed the Kanban methodology because the business was not functioning well during the 1940s when compared to the competitors in America. Kanban helped Toyota control the systems involved in the production of their automobiles, which improved productivity. The Kanban method also helped the business reduce the amount of raw material that went to waste.

A Kanban system controls the value chain. It starts with the supplier of raw material and ends at the customer. This makes it easier for teams to avoid any disruptions in the supply chain functioning, and also reduces the excess of any inventory at different steps of the process. The Kanban method requires constant monitoring, and the project manager must identify any bottlenecks in the system. Since most companies want to achieve high output with low delivery times, they should choose the Kanban project management methodology since that helps to improve efficiency.

What is the Kanban Method?

As mentioned earlier, the Kanban method was developed by Taiichi Ohno to improve the manufacturing process in Toyota. David Anderson used this methodology in the IT industry for software development in 2004. He then went on to define the method using concepts like queuing theory, pull systems, and flow using the work by Eli Goldratt, Peter Drucker, Edward Demmings, Taiichi Ohno, and others.

Kanban Change Management Principles

The Kanban methodology uses a list of principles and practices that help to manage or improve the workflow. This method is evolutionary and non-disruptive and helps to improve any process being performed in the organization or any project. You, as a project manager, can implement the principles and practices of Kanban to improve every step in the business process. You can improve the workflow by reducing the time spent on completing the task, increasing customer satisfaction, and maximizing every team member's capabilities. Now, look at some of the foundational principles and practices of the Kanban methodology.

Foundational Principles

Always start with what you are doing now

When you implement the Kanban methodology, you do not have to make any changes to the processes immediately. You should, instead, focus on the current workflow and look for the sections where you can make some improvements wherever needed. You must also ensure that your team members accept the changes that you make to the process.

Pursue Evolutionary and Incremental Change

The Kanban methodology allows every member of the project team to make some changes to the process. Since they work together with the project manager to make these changes, there will be very little resistance from the team and the organization.

Respect Current Roles, Responsibilities, and Designations

Unlike other project management methodologies, the Kanban methodology does not require the organization to change the structure. The business does not have to make any changes to existing functions and roles that are not performing well. The only processes that must be changed, if necessary, are the tasks or processes within the project.

Encourage Acts of Leadership

The Kanban methodology encourages continuous improvement to processes at every level in the organization. People at any level are allowed to lead the change or identify some improvements to the processes. They are always encouraged to identify ways to improve the processes followed to meet the objectives of any project.

Core Practices

Visualize the Workflow

When you begin to implement the Kanban methodology, you should visualize the workflow of the tasks. You should visualize the steps in the workflow on the Kanban board, so you know the steps that must be followed to complete the task. The Kanban board can either be simple or complex based on the different types of items or tasks in the workflow that the team should deliver.

Once the team and the project manager visualize the process, it is important to visualize the current work that is being done by the team. The team can do this by using different cards or colors to identify the different classes of work. You should also include different colors and columns to define the tasks or processes, which the team works on. It is a good idea to use a Kanban board, which can help to redesign the process.

Limit or Reduce Work-in-Progress

It is important to limit work-in-progress to implement the Kanban system. This will encourage your team to complete work that is ongoing before taking up any new project. It means that the team can only take up a new process when work that is in progress is marked complete. This increases the team's capacity to bring in more work.

It may not be easy to identify the limit of work-in-progress. You may begin with no WIP limits, and author Donald G. Reinertsen had suggested that a team should start with no WIP limits and then observe how the team performs when you begin to use Kanban. When you have sufficient data, you can define your WIP limits at every stage of the workflow. Most teams start with a WIP limit that is either 1 or 1.5 times the number of people in the team working on a specific task.

It is beneficial to the team to limit WIP and put WIP limits since the team members will finish their tasks before they move on to new tasks. This also communicates to the stakeholders and customers that there is a limited capacity of work that can be performed by the team. Therefore, careful planning must be involved when any new task or request is made to the team.

Manage Flow

Once you implement the first two activities on this list, you should work on managing and improving the workflow. The Kanban methodology will help the project manager handle the workflow by splitting the workflow into stages and also understand the status of every task. The WIP limit will be set based on the tasks in the workflow. Every member of the team will work on completing the tasks within the WIP limits set since they know that the work will be piled up if there is any task that is held up. This will affect the speed at which the work can be delivered.

The Kanban methodology will help the project manager and the team analyze the system, and also adjust some tasks in the workflow. It will also allow the team to understand how they can spend time efficiently to complete a task. It is important to look at the intermediate stages to observe the tasks, identify bottlenecks, and resolve those bottlenecks in the workflow. Teams should always analyze the time that a task stays in the intermediate stage and identify some ways to reduce the time spent on those stages. This is an important step that one should consider if the team wants to reduce the time spent on the project.

Once the workflow improves, the team will learn to deliver any project smoothly. When the team is more predictable, they will become more comfortable to realize the commitments that are made to the customers and also complete the work within the set timelines. Teams should always forecast completion times, which will help them improve the functionality of the team.

Make Policies Explicit

The team should work on defining the policies explicitly. They should also find a way to visualize those policies so they can explain the work that is being done in the process. A project manager should always create the policy and define the amount of work the team should complete. The policies can always be written at a broad level. These policies can also include some checklists, which must be ticked off at the end of every task to ensure that the team is meeting all the required criteria. These lists should be made for every task that the team performs to ensure that the team maintains the workflow. For instance, the project manager should include the definition of when the task is complete or understand whether a task is pushed or pulled in the policies.

Feedback Loops

It is important to include feedback loops in any system, and the Kanban methodology requires every member of the team to implement a constructive feedback loop. The team, as a whole, should look at the different stages in the process on the board. They can then use the information on the board to generate metrics and reports that can be used to improve the process.

Most teams do not understand the mantra "Fail fast and fail often," and this may not work for most teams. Having said that, this method would make it easier for the project manager and the team to identify any issues at the start so that the process has fewer errors. It is important for every team to have a feedback loop in the process.

Improve and Evolve Collaboratively and Experimentally

The Kanban methodology is an improvement process that allows teams and people to make changes to the processes before they make a huge improvement. This will make it easier for teams to implement the changes quickly. The Kanban methodology allows members to use statistical methods where the members can build a hypothesis and test that hypothesis to understand that outcome.

Teams need to evaluate a process and then improve the process wherever necessary. It is important to observe these changed processes and assess the impact of that change on the process using the Kanban board. These results will help the project manager and teams evaluate if the change made to the process is improving the process or not, and decide to keep the change or remove it.

The Kanban methodology helps a team collect all the information required to assess the performance of the process and also every member of the team. This data makes it easier for the project manager to generate the necessary metrics to evaluate the performance and tweak any other processes if needed.

Implementing Kanban

When it comes to implementing Kanban, you must ensure that you have enough patience since the implementation of Kanban is a continuous process. That said, the results will never disappoint you. Most project managers use the steps mentioned below to implement the Kanban methodology in their company or project.

Step One: Visualization Of Workflow

This is the most important step that you will need to perform when you implement the Kanban methodology. Remember that the Kanban method is primarily based on visualization. Therefore, you will need to create the Kanban task board first when you choose to implement this methodology. You can either use a physical or digital board since there is no difference between the two. The principle of the board is the same. This board should represent the stages or the status of every task like "to do", "in progress", or "done". The tasks should then be placed under these statuses depending on the stages.

Step Two: Limit the Amount of WIP

As mentioned earlier, one of the main principles of Kanban is to limit the number of tasks in the work-in-progress stage. You must limit the number of tasks that you work on when you implement Kanban, which will make it easier for you to spend your time efficiently. Some believe that it is a good idea to handle multiple processes or tasks at once, but this is not the case in Kanban. You can only use Kanban if you limit or reduce the number of units or tasks at the work-in-progress stage.

Step Three: Switch to Explicit Policies

In this step, you should plan the entire project. You should understand the project well and identify the objectives and target goals. This will help you predict the project in the right manner.

Step Four: Measure and Manage the Workflow

If you want to improve the quality of your product and also increase the time you spend on creating the product, you should use a Kanban cycle.

Step Five: Using Scientific Methods for Optimization

You should use the Kanban board to create a new strategy. You should make some changes to the strategies that you use if you wish to improve the workflow. You can predict the changes in the workflow and the results if you use the Kanban task board. This will help you create your approach to complete the project.

Conclusion

Lean thinking and agile are a way of business and not just methods used to improve projects. Some businesses have dived into these approaches and use lean thinking and agile methods to improve businesses and processes. Both lean and agile project management methodologies will require a change to be made to the processes and also to the management and leadership. This is the only way the business will be open to new ideas and thoughts.

These new-age project management methodologies will make it easier for businesses to encourage their employees to identify new ways to improve processes, innovate and develop new processes, and identify issues and develop solutions to cater to those issues. This creates a sense of equality in the organization since every employee has the right to voice his or her opinion. It is important that you establish these processes in the firm right from the beginning to foster a sense of inclusion and innovation.

It is hard to identify the right method for your team at the first attempt. You will also take some time to get the hang of the process. Make sure that you understand the concepts well before you implement them in your organization or team. Remember that you cannot afford to make a mistake with implementation since that will cost the company a lot of money and time.

Thank you for purchasing this book. I hope you have gathered all the necessary information.

Part 2: Lean Six Sigma

A Practical Guide for Getting Started with Lean Six Sigma along with How It Can Be Integrated with Agile and Scrum

Introduction

For every business, there's always room to do better, always room to be more productive, and to make more profit. And there's always room to waste less time and resources. Although many business owners possess excellent skills in their various industries, many are oblivious regarding properly managing projects and achieving the best results. Thus, to fill this gap, they seek out new human capital to help them do that. Specifically, they are on the search for talented project managers. These are project managers who aren't only aware of the traditional way of performing projects, but who also have experience in the new methodologies too. They're aware that most projects are filled with waste and inefficiencies. How do they know this? They're equipped with the right knowledge about Lean Six Sigma.

So, what is Lean Six Sigma all about? Lean Six Sigma is a globally proven and applied methodology that delivers a demonstrable and sustainable improvement of processes and organizations. The focus is on matters *that matter to customers*. This methodology leads to simultaneously reducing costs, increasing customer satisfaction, and shortening lead time. This involves investing in human capital and making optimal use of people's knowledge and skills for cost-effective and successful projects. Lean Six Sigma offers a framework with which organizations can achieve concrete results with continuous improvement in a structured manner. Implementing Lean Six Sigma gives an organization a goal-oriented approach by translating the strategy into tangible results. Lean Six Sigma projects ensure a sustainable improvement of the operating result. Business problems are solved better and permanently. The return on investment (ROI) of a Lean Six Sigma process varies - but is usually multifold of what was invested.

The basis for Lean Six Sigma is data and facts. This concerns both making the results measurable, providing insight into the real wishes of the customers, reliably measuring current performance, and objectively testing the root causes. In this way, you can tell if the solutions being implemented have the desired effects. Both Lean and Six Sigma started as separate methodologies. Lean strives for more transfer and value generation, while Six Sigma strives for stable and effective processes. In combination, they reinforce each other and are entirely complimentary. Organizations are confronted with rising costs and increasing competition on a day to day basis, but using the Lean and Six Sigma combination, you can combat these problems and grow your business. There are great benefits found in this methodology, such as an increase in profits, improved efficiency and effectiveness, lower costs, and support for employees to develop their skills and knowledge.

It's deplorable that many project managers spend a lot of time and energy working toward ill-defined project goals. These goals don't matter to the organization and are poorly stipulated because no time was taken out to define what's really important to customers and, thus, the organization. To remain concise, many project managers fail to understand the intricate difference between efficiency and effectiveness. When an organization is efficient, this means getting as much done as possible in as little amount of time. But the mantra of "doing more with less" is pointless without direction, i.e., effectiveness. When an organization is effective, this means that they are moving forward on the right path and *know their destination*.

While traversing this right path, successful organizations aim to do more with fewer resources, like time and money.

All of this talk about Lean Six Sigma may sound too good to be true for you as a new or aspiring project manager. However, it's real, and many organizations around the world are proving it to be an effective and powerful program. Although much has been written about project management, too much information is too generic and not applicable in today's ever-changing world. Thus, this guide was written to cover all aspects and processes of Lean Six Sigma in a secure and up-to-date manner. Besides, this book contains simple language and no fluff, so every beginner can follow along without losing track of its main points. Due to the lack of practical guides on the topic, my aim in this book is to share with you as many practical examples, case studies, and expert advice you need to start applying the concepts right away. The examples, case studies, and specialist advice are distilled from my experience managing projects and from other very successful project managers. So, even more seasoned project managers can benefit from this book. All this results in a comprehensive book on the topic; you don't need any additional material to get started. Finally, the guide is also suited for those who want to pursue a Lean Six Sigma Certification - or aren't yet sure if they're going to acquire one.

This book consists of two primary parts, namely: The Essentials and The Process. Within these recipes, we find various ingredients needed to make the "correct meal." Without a guide, without the right elements, it's impossible to complete a project successfully. The first part, The Essentials, is covered in Chapters 1-4. In Chapter 1, I'll explain more about what Lean Project Management is all about. By reading this chapter, you'll learn more about its origins, processes, and principles. In Chapter 2, you'll have a solid understanding of the various tools, roles, and concepts within the Six Sigma framework. This is related to Chapter 3, wherein I explain the Lean Six Sigma methodology and benefits in beginner-friendly language. To finish this first part, Chapter 4 gives you a view about training and certifications and answers the question of whether you need one.

The second part, The Process, is covered in chapters 5-12. This part is all about the practical process of Lean Six Sigma. In chapter 5, we'll delve deep into the Lean Six Sigma Process and what DMAIC and DMADV are all about. Afterward, Chapters 6-10, are all dedicated to the various phases in Lean Six Sigma, namely the Define, Measure, Analyze, Improve, and control phases.

Furthermore, in Chapters 11, I'll give you more information about the relation between Lean Six Sigma, Agile, and Scrum. Finally, in Chapter 12, you'll learn more about mistakes to avoid when implementing Lean Six Sigma. I'll explain the secrets of how to properly combine Lean Six Sigma with the very practical Agile approach to prevent many of these mistakes. This will set you up for more success in projects. So, are you ready to uncover these secrets and grab the necessary techniques? Let's go!

Chapter 1. What is Lean Project Management?

The rise of new technologies has brought much dynamicity in the work we do. Because of the dynamic environment organizations function in today, we not appropriate ways to manage this dynamicity. Traditional project methodologies, like the Waterfall Method, aren't very feasible with rapidly changing customer needs and wishes. Fortunately, with the rise of software development, great minds came together to craft an approach to better manage projects. This resulted in approaches like Agile and Lean. Agile brings about many benefits, consider the following:

> • **It results in shorter lead times.** In the past, an IT project consisted of a lengthy, usually unrealistic planning. If one part was canceled or if the planning had to be revised for another reason, this would entail a lot of trouble. Often, the result was very different from what was intended. Then the whole project - or significant parts of the project - would start again, often with a considerable lead time as a result. The Agile approach ensures considerably less administration because you only have to adjust the following sprint (defined time to deliver a product increment) instead of the entire

project planning. This makes the lead time of the total project a lot shorter.

- **It paves the way for better customer satisfaction.** With traditional project management methodologies, the customer was involved in the kick-off and delivery. However, the process in between determined whether the result was according to the original plan. In Agile, the customer remains involved throughout the entire process and provides input and feedback during every sprint. Thus, it is continuously checked whether all stakeholders are on the same line. This ensures higher customer satisfaction.

- **It results in better, higher quality projects.** If you work with Agile, you gradually process feedback and customer wishes in your project. In the scrum method, a (partial) product is delivered after every sprint. Everything is also tested, and errors and deviations are quickly discovered. You can guarantee that the end product not only resembles the original plan but also works properly. With the Agile approach, you increase the quality of your solution. You provide the customer with real added value.

- **It lowers risks and costs.** Agile is a type of risk management because there's always room to readjust. The constant feedback received from customers and the higher quality of the delivered incremental products reduce the risk of errors and loss of resources.

- **More teamwork.** Working incrementally towards a common goal results in close cooperation between all disciplines, such as business analysts and software developers. There is complete transparency about what each team member does and at what time. There is more focus, no unnecessary meetings, and you see a ton of quick wins resulting from the team's efforts. This ensures more satisfaction and motivation for the entire team.

The Agile approach has brought various methodologies for better managing projects, such as *Lean*. Lean means slim. By employing Lean, organizations and businesses, make their processes "slimmer." This means that all wastage, "the unnecessary excess fats," are eliminated. With *waste*, we refer to elements for which the customer doesn't want to pay or wait; things that offer no added value to the customer, such as when a manufacturing worker needs to walk to the other side of the factory to grab some equipment. With Lean, everyone within the company can respond quickly and perform optimally. It consists of these key elements:

- Make sure to reduce stock
- Hyper-focus on reducing the lead time
- Strive for as much flow and least "hiccups" in the process as possible, creating flow in the process;
- Create a sense of *Pull*;
- Always aim and go for perfection.

The central idea within the Lean methodology is to put customers first and create more value for them with minimal effort. This approach helps you achieve increased customer satisfaction, employee satisfaction, and continuous quality improvement. Applying the Lean methodology brings your processes in an optimal form to reach peak performance and not get "exhausted." With Lean, a company produces both more efficiently and more sustainably. A more efficient production process that has been optimized through Lean uses fewer materials and energy per production unit. This is due to far less downtime and fewer decoupling stocks.

Although Lean started in the automotive industry, today its used in all kinds of industries, from IT companies to clothing manufacturers. If you decide to implement Lean Management in your business or organization, awareness, and acceptance of your team members is essential to reach the desired outcomes. These elements will be explained in more detail later on. However, remember that no process, organization, or culture is the same. There's always a certain degree of adjustments needed to make the best use of Lean. Usually, it's taking one step back to take two steps forward. Let's now take a step back and learn how Lean started before we delve into further intricacies!

The Origins of Lean

Lean is, by far, the most used methodology to improve processes. But what are its origins? How did it come about? Who used it first? To answer these questions and more, we need to take a step back in history, back to the end of the nineteenth century. An entrepreneur and Japanese inventor, Sakichi Toyoda developed a mechanical loom. That kicked off a textile industry revolution in Japan, and in January 1918, he started his company, the Toyoda Spinning and Weaving Company. His son, Kiichiro Toyoda, helped and, although there were many setbacks, by 1924, his dream came alive, and he could finish constructing an automatic loom. In 1926, Toyoda Automatic Loom Works was opened.

To do all of this, Toyoda made good use of the Jikoda Principles, the main one of which stood for incorporating quality automatically into the main objective, i.e., production, free of defects, and removing any redundancies. Later, Sakichi was to make a change to the name of his company, calling it "Toyota."

The family didn't stop there, though. As an inventor, his son made many visits to the US and Europe in the 1920s, and it was there that he met the automotive industry. When Sakichi Toyoda sold the patent to the automatic loom, his son used the money to set down the foundations for a new company. In 1937, the Toyota Motor Corporation was born, and Kiirichi began to produce the company's first vehicles, using General Motors parts. One of his most important legacies was the Toyota Production System. Kiichiro's "just-in-time" philosophy - production of only the exact amount of parts already ordered striving for minimal waste - was an essential factor in the development of this system. The Toyota Production System was slowly but surely being used by more and more car manufacturers throughout the world.

After the Second World War, a cousin of Toyoda's, Eiji Toyoda, who now also worked for Toyota, visited Michigan. Here he attended the Ford factory in Dearborn to study their method of production. On his return, he discovered that the way Ford manufactured cars wasn't feasible in Japan, because of the smaller market. Thus, the company searched for an alternative way of manufacturing, which turned out to be utterly different from Ford's highly effective mass production system. When Japan began to pick itself up after the industrial chaos of the war, Toyota became the largest Japanese automobile manufacturer, having a current market share of around 42%. At the end of the fifties, Toyota delved into various regions. The first Toyota Crown vehicles arrived in the US in 1957. And in 1965, with models like the Toyota Corolla, the company started to build a reputation and sell numbers that could compete with those of local producers.

This was never possible without the alternative the company found. They shifted their focus on an entirely new way of producing with attention to development, manufacturing, delivery, assembly, and of course, labor. This new approach is named the Toyota Production System. The following four Ps can describe the basis for this system:

- **Problem-solving is first and foremost.** While producing cars, we have to learn and continuously improve the processes to gain the best results.

- **People & Partners are critical to success.** Without the right partners, processes cannot run. If a partner slacks down, the whole process slacks down. Therefore, great partners are needed who give great attention to transparency: hard work, and collaboration.

- **Process(es) run the production.** A system is based on a multitude of processes. Problems in one process can have a direct effect on another process. Thus, dealing with them in a professional or entrepreneurial way is necessary.

- **Philosophy keeps us on track.** Without the right philosophy, nothing worthwhile can be achieved. Thus, focusing on instilling long-term thinking, great collaboration, a clear mission, and vision in every team member is critical.

The term Lean was first championed in the west by John Krafcik in his paper *Triumph of the Lean Production System* (1988). In the paper, Krafcik gives more insights into productivity and quality levels in the auto industry. Before his research, people in the auto industry believed that an assembly plant's location determines productivity and quality levels. He concluded that plants operating with a more *Lean* approach could produce motor vehicles faster while retaining high levels of productivity and quality. In 1990, James Womack, Daniel Jones, and Daniel Roos wrote the book *The Machine That Changed the World*. It discusses a study they conducted into the difference in effectiveness between various car manufacturers. They found that Toyota was first and foremost in the global automobile branch, because of the Lean production principles they applied. These principles were later detailed in a paper written in 1996 by James Womack and Daniel Jones, called *Lean Thinking: Banish Waste and Create Wealth in Your* Corporation. The principles mentioned in the article were detailed further in their book with the same title. By now, I hope I made you more curious about these principles that made Toyota extremely successful in their industry. Let's take a closer look.

Lean Principles and Benefits

Now that we've taken a look at the origins of Lean, what are these principles all about I mentioned previously? According to James Womack and Daniel Jones, there are five principles of Lean Thinking, namely:

- Specify Value;

- Identify the Value Stream;
- Flow;
- Pull;
- Pursue Perfection.

Lean Management focuses on removing waste from processes. This results in working smarter, not necessarily harder, to better serve your customers. It doesn't matter in what industry you'd like to apply Lean; it's beneficial for pretty much every industry and company size. To turn your organization into a Lean organization, understanding and to apply the principles mentioned above helps you build a strong foundation. Let's take a closer look at each principle.

The first principle is defining or specifying *value* by putting first things first, i.e., your customers. A business is nothing without customers, depending on them and growing because of them. So, this makes it seem quite important. And, indeed, it's quite important. This begs the questions why a lot of companies don't ask more questions related to their customers instead of their competitors. Think of questions like, "In what way can we create as much value as possible for our customers?" Value is a process or service (or a part of it) that the customer pays or waits for. Before we can even attempt to answer the question, you need a clear view of who your customer is, to begin with. Are your customers predominantly female, between the ages 30-50, and do they like to read? These customer characteristics should be taken into consideration. To better frame your ideal customer, you can make a persona. A persona is a detailed description of a user of your product or service. Although personas are based on fictional characters, their specifications are based on real data gathered through talking with customers.

Furthermore, don't forget that customers aren't always external, you can have internal customers too, such as colleagues from a different department. It may seem common sense to focus on the customer to properly define value, but what is common sense isn't common practice. How often are things done "because they always went this way," "because the boss wants it" or "because we think the customer wants it"? Without a doubt, when you don't know what your customer wants, there's no way to manage anything adequately. Don't misinterpret customer value from customer demand. Although the difference may seem subtle, don't overlook it! Customer-centric companies understand extremely well what is of value to their (potential) customers. Thus, they "surprise" customers with a product that they had not yet asked for, but turned out to be of great value. For example, take Amazon, who started selling books and obsessively listens to customer's needs and desires. The customers wanted a wide range of books to pick and wanted these delivered as soon as possible. Amazon did exactly that by broadening the number of books available through its platform and building more fulfillment centers to ship the products to customers quicker. Thus, Amazon's revenue grew steadily, making it easier for them to "surprise" their (potential) customers with new gadgets, such as the Kindle and Alexa.

The second principle is about *identifying the value stream*; we need to determine where value is created. This can only be done after you have a clear image of the customer you want to serve and what they perceive as value and whatnot. Afterward, you take a look at your organization and see which activities add value to the customer and which do not. The second category, matters that don't add value to the customer, is called *waste* in the Lean methodology. A useful technique to make this evident is called *value stream mapping*. Thereby, you can map and detail processes and process steps from the trigger of the customer to the delivery of a service or product. Next, by taking a critical look at the created *value stream map*, we can determine for specific activities if they add value to the customer or not. So, we ask if *the customer value-added* or not. Lean distinguishes the activities that the customer doesn't value into two groups:

- Activities that add value to the business (Business Value Added): These are activities needed to keep the business going. You should minimize this as much as possible.

- Activities that add no value to the business (Non-Value Added): These activities are a complete waste of time and worthless. They aren't of value to the customer. First and foremost, and not to your business. What do we do with these? If possible, we want to eliminate them. Otherwise, we try to bring these worthless activities to a minimum.

To further illustrate this, say we run a marketing agency and want to give our clients more insights into market statistics. Delivering a short presentation with critical findings creates value for the clients. Now, before we could give this presentation, we had to be compliant with laws and regulations. Although being compliant isn't directly part of the value creation toward the client, it was necessary to do matters that create value, in this case, the presentation. However, if the presentation software we use crashes every couple of minutes, this is of no benefit to both the customer and the organization. Thus, this waste should be eliminated or reduced as much as possible.

The third principle *flow* is about ensuring a continuous flow in processes. This principle follows the previous step seamlessly because it focuses on removing all identified wastes from the process. By doing so, nothing remains but the value-adding activities. The next step is to adjust these activities to one another so that no congestion arises, and thus a natural flow is created. The ultimate Lean solution is the application of what professionals call a "one-piece flow," whereby (in contrast to batch production) valuable stocks are kept to a minimum, and errors or mistakes aren't passed on to the next process step. However, in practice, a more hybrid approach is, in many cases, the right solution. The purpose of creating this flow is to have the service or product "flow" to the customer according to her/his requirements without wasting time. This is only possible if the employees of an organization think from the chain of activities instead of seeing everything in separate boxes, i.e., looking at it in a vacuum. By making the lead time of the chain as short as possible, it's more the standard than the exception to have online orders reach customers the next day. Where "same-day delivery" is now something unique, this might be the standard sooner rather than later, because of the continuous improvement companies pursue in terms of shortening their lead time.

The fourth principle *pull* is all about doing what is needed when it's needed. With the previous steps, we've minimized the waste within the business process. Also, the processes are now far more focused on adding value to the customer, but something is missing, namely producing or delivering the service when the customer requests it. This limits unnecessary intermediate and final stocks. The outflow of products is the trigger for the organization to ensure new inflow. Of course, this principle doesn't mean that there isn't any stock at all. Take Walmart as an example. If the Walmart employees had to bake something like bread from scratch on the spot, that would take a lot of time, resulting in tremendous waste. Instead, *Pull* means that Walmart knows very precisely how much stock they need to keep. Thereby, they can replenish this stock based on previous sales data, *just-in-time*. According to Cambridge Dictionary, "a just-in-time system of manufacturing is based on preventing waste by producing only the amounts of goods(/products) needed at a particular time, and not paying to produce and store more goods than are needed."

The fifth principle *of perfection* is related to continuously learning and improving. With the rise of online communication channels, we're bombarded with messages and posts, wherever you go or don't go. Some posts proclaim that we shouldn't strive for perfection. Doing so would be mission impossible and would only result in distress, anxiety, and maybe a burnout. Why? Because perfection is something we'll never achieve with our fallibility. Therefore, this is not the idea behind this principle. The goal is to be a learning organization that does a little better day after day instead of large, usually uncertain, improvements now and then. A useful tool is organizing a weekly consultation or daily standup to structure the week or day's work. This makes daily improvement more ingrained in employees. Besides, it helps to ensure further improvements so that the chance for waste is eliminated or reduced to a minimum.

Lean Benefits and Waste

In the previous paragraph, we learned more about the various principles and that Lean is about creating more value for customers and eliminate or reduce all forms of waste. Lean distinguishes seven types of waste, often referred to with the acronym TIM WOOD(S), namely:

- **T**ransport. Moving products or materials (raw materials, documents, work in progress) between operations. Also, think of things like being physically separated from successive processes or an illogical layout of the workplace. Transport must be minimized because it takes time in which no value can be added and because products can be damaged during transport.

- **I**nventory. Keeping stocks of material and products, such as unread emails, pending customer cases, pending requests, or spare parts that are never used.

- **M**ovement. Any physical movement that does not add value to the process. Think of matters like unnecessary walking, lifting, turning, or reaching due to, for instance, the incorrect layout of the workplace or to search for documents.

- **W**aiting. Man or machine must wait for the completion of the previous process step. Waiting for authorization, starting a software program, instructions, and information are all examples.

- **O**verproduction. Producing more than necessary and doing more than requested by the customer. Also, things such as producing more information or documents than necessary, doing too much, starting too early or producing too quickly.

This leads to stockpiling, yields nothing, costs time, space, and often requires management or maintenance.

• **O**verprocessing. Perform more process steps than necessary for the minimum for order handling. For instance, making the product "more beautiful" than strictly necessary, doing more than what the customer wants, such as picking up things outside the agreed standard service, doing things twice (saving files both physically and electronically), et cetera.

• **D**efects. This is the correction of mistakes made. For example, outages or errors, products or parts of services that do not meet the specifications of the customer, and incomplete or incorrect information.

• The seven wastes mentioned above are widely known in the Lean community. However, many organizations saw the need for an eight form of waste, namely, **S**kills. This is about the under-utilization of human potential due to the incomplete use of knowledge and creativity. Examples of this are over-qualified or under-qualified staff, too little use of employee capacities (an employee has a certain skill set that's untapped), and delegating tasks to employees with insufficient training.

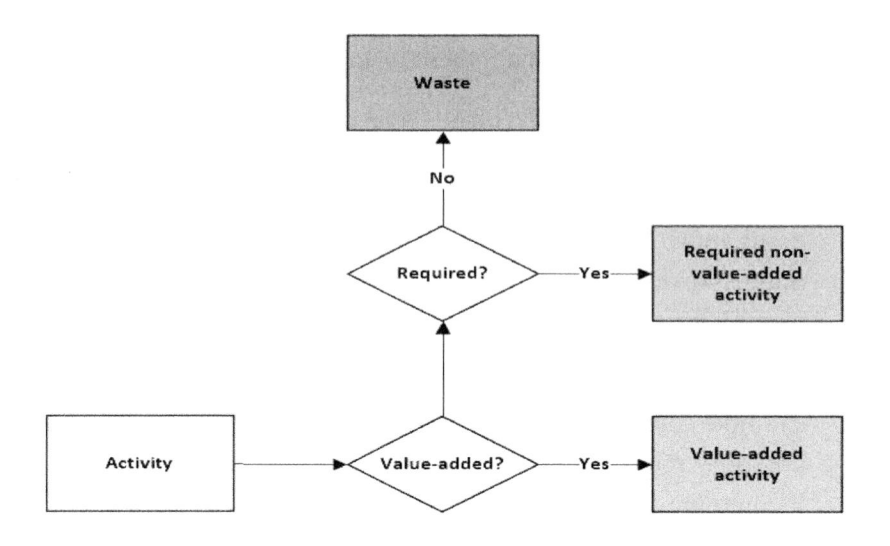

Image of a flowchart that starts with activity as a process. Then we check if it's value-added. If the answer is "Yes," this would be a value-added activity. If the answer is "No," it could be either a required non-value-added activity if it were necessary and a waste if it weren't necessary.

In later chapters, these wastes will be addressed further. But before we continue to the next chapters, it's good to provide you with a summary of the benefits we addressed in this chapter.

One of the greatest benefits that these Lean principles bring about is that they help you save a lot of time. This time can then be used to engage with customers to find new needs or wishes to create, keep, and deliver more value in a better fashion. Thus, the last principle of *perfection* brings us back to the first principle *value* to complete the circle. The principles mentioned above all bring about great benefits. In terms of the first principle *value*, a great benefit is that we always put the customer first. This has been the core of many successful businesses we hear about today, such as Amazon and Google. Putting customers first, has in and of itself a myriad of benefits, such as increasing customer satisfaction, turning more prospects into paying customers, and (usually) making more profit in the long term. Regarding the second principle *value stream*, a great benefit is that we create a vivid image of how processes run. With this knowledge, it's possible to identify bottlenecks, tackle these, whereby we create more efficient business processes. The third principle *flow* has many benefits too. For instance, if the processes run smoothly and don't inherit flaws from other processes, this will lead to reduced costs. Besides, the fourth principle *pull* shows us that doing more with less would benefit our business in the long run. Why? Because when we only do what is needed when it's needed, we drastically reduce the complexity of delivering our products and/or services. Finally, the fifth principle *of perfection*, has a lot of benefits as well, such as increased team morale. If you want to retain the great talent you've acquired, you need to challenge these professionals continually. If the work becomes boring or redundant, they'll easily leave you for a place where they can grow and are challenged more. When small improvements or "quick wins" are amplified in a talented team, it wants to strive to gain more and push new frontiers. In the end, this will create more value for the organization, but most importantly, more value for the customer.

Chapter 2. Six Sigma: Tools, Roles, and Concepts

In the previous chapter, we've addressed Lean. In this chapter, we'll take a look at Six Sigma. Six Sigma is the most effective methodology for problem-solving and improving the performance of business processes and the organization. All business, technical, or process challenges are far easier to overcome with the help of the Six Sigma methodology. The world's largest businesses have used Six Sigma to increase their combined profits by billions of dollars year after year, the past decade. Nowadays, in an increasing amount of organizations, competency of Six Sigma is necessary for any managerial position. Fortune 500 companies were first and foremost in adapting the principles of this methodology. In the past, it was always difficult for small and medium-sized businesses, public institutions, non-profit organizations, educational institutions, and even ambitious individuals to properly implement Six Sigma. This was mainly due to the scarcity of people experienced in this area. Most of these experts would be hired by large corporations who could pay the greatest sums. Fortunately, nowadays, things are different as the methods and tools of Six Sigma spread; more information about it was shared. Thus, it became easier to understand and easier to implement.

Simply put, Six Sigma is about applying a structured scientific method to improve an aspect of an organization, process, or person. It's about performing data collection and analysis, which helps you identify the best possible ways to meet your customers' needs and satisfy the organization's needs while minimizing wasted resources and maximizing profits. Six Sigma can be used anywhere. It's not only applicable in large and complex companies, but also the less complex and smaller businesses. Six Sigma is a rigorous and structured approach to problem-solving, for which you record data and apply statistical analyses to find out the real causes of the challenges that you encounter in production, service, or even transaction environments. That is why various chapters in this book describe and define various statistical tools of Six Sigma. But don't worry, these concepts will be explained in easy-to-understand language even if you don't know anything about statistics.

So, what's up with the name Six Sigma, you might think? You may know that sigma is the eighteenth letter of the Greek alphabet. But did you know that the term "six sigma" is used as it described a target of 3.4 defects per million opportunities? This small amount of defects in processes is near-perfect and considered world-class by organizations worldwide. Around 6 standard deviations around a central tendency covers this world-class result, namely 99,99966 percent accuracy (3.4 / 1.000.000 (x 100%) = 0.00034%, then subtract 100% from it). If the aforementioned standard deviations have a place within the specified customer requirements, we can confidently say that the process is Six Sigma competent. Through the years, this methodology has evolved to the point where it now contains several distinct aspects. These are listed below:

- First, as I just explained, Six Sigma performance is the statistical term for a process that produces fewer than 3.4 defects/mistakes per million defect options.

- Secondly, the methodology is about solving issues. Many organizations even see it as the most effective method for problem-solving when it comes to improving the performance of the business and organization.

• Third, a Six Sigma competent improvement occurs when the most critical outcomes of a business or work process are improved to a significant degree, usually by seventy percent or more.

• Fourth, an organization that strives to become Six Sigma oriented uses the methods and tools of Six Sigma to improve its performance by continuously reducing costs, increasing revenue, increasing customer satisfaction, expanding capacity and capabilities, reducing complexity, shorten the cycle time, and limit defects and errors.

• Fifth, proper execution is the prescribed roll-out of the Six Sigma methodology within an organization, with methods, roles, and procedures that are determined by generally accepted standards.

These aspects are closely related to the fundamental concepts within Six Sigma, with an order of importance; these are the following:

• The first key concept has *stable operations*. With this concept, Six Sigma organizations focus on ensuring foreseeable and unchanging processes to better the customer experience.

• The second key concept is called *critical to quality*. This is about the internal critical quality parameters that relate to the wishes and needs of the customer.

• The third key concept is the *process capability*. This is a measure of the ability of a process to produce consistent results. It's the ratio between the allowable distribution and the actual distribution of the results of a process. In short, it makes clear what your process can deliver.

- The fourth key concept is *a defect* and is any kind of unwanted result for your organization, but especially your customer. Because of the customer-centric view, it's generally defined as an error that means that at least one of the criteria for acceptance by your customers has not been met.

- The fifth key concept is *variation*. This is a statistical measure for the spread or variation. With this measurement, we get a better image of what the customer can sense, in particular, what she/he can see and feel.

- The sixth key concept is *design for Six Sigma* and is based on the premise that what we do as an organization is first cross-examined with what is best for the customer. Processes in your organization have to be designed in such a way that makes room for doing the same, i.e., meeting the wishes and desires of your target audience.

Knowing these critical concepts makes it easier for us to debunk the myths surrounding them. Just take people who say that Six Sigma only focuses on reducing defects. Well, this is far from the truth, because of the critical concepts, others don't deal directly with defects, such as *variation*. But why would we even care about defending Six Sigma, let alone apply it? Well, not using the concepts it contains causes many organizations to lose as much as twenty to thirty percent of their profits through mistakes that could've been prevented. This is a grave penalty for not working effectively and efficiently. Just imagine you had to throw thirty percent of your salary in the trash, every single month. This may seem outrageous, but this is exactly what most businesses do! Therefore, a good understanding of Six Sigma will benefit you, your organization, and your customers. So, let's take a step back and go to the time where it all began.

The Origins of Six Sigma

In the previous chapter, we took a look at Lean and how it originated. As you might've noticed, in this chapter, we addressed Six Sigma. Therefore, it seems logical to me to address its beginnings as well.

The start of Six Sigma came from the mathematician Carl Frederick Gauss. Gauss introduced the concept of the normal distribution, whereby the average spread of a measured value around a target value is expressed in the standard deviation. Six Sigma is a less accessible methodology than Lean due to the many statistical components that require more time. However, the method can be used in all kinds of industries. It's ultimately about customers and what they find important. Therefore, it's always good to first identify the wishes and needs of your customers through market research before you get started with Six Sigma. Six Sigma makes the probability that products and / or services are in accordance with what the customer wants as high as possible. Thus, customers are less likely to be disappointed. Although Six Sigma involves some statistics, by no means do you have to be a math genius to apply Six Sigma. Gauss did not come up with the exact method, but with his calculations, he laid the foundation for making variations in processes measurable.

Six Sigma is a management strategy that was originally developed by the American multinational communication company Motorola. Six Sigma, as a true management strategy, came to life at Motorola in the 1980s. The credits for Six Sigma as an improvement tool went to Motorola engineer Bill Smith when the company achieved a ten times reduction in product failure levels in a couple of years, something unheard of before. Unfortunately, Smith wasn't able to witness the hype around Six Sigma, because he passed away in 1993 in the Motorola cafeteria due to a heart attack. But this didn't stop the methodology from growing even further. Six Sigma matured further in large companies such as General Electric (GE), which managed to garner considerable savings by applying it. Soon after, General Electric became one of the most important users.

The same method is now used in pretty much any industry you could think of. Six Sigma has grown into a process management method that can be used in many different situations. Increasingly, Six Sigma is used by service companies, for example, by IT companies and transportation businesses. Six Sigma is particularly suitable for solving problems where the cause is not immediately apparent. A condition for this is that the quality of the relevant product and / or process must be measurable. Then the factors that influence the quality the most are improved. The most important approach of Six Sigma is quality management and the reduction of variation in production and business processes. Besides, discovering defects or errors and removing them is also important with Six Sigma. Therefore, the method consists of a collection of quality management methods. A Six Sigma project within an organization follows a certain sequence of steps in advance and also has financial objectives. These are five steps, which together form the acronym DMAIC, which stands for Define, Measure, Analyze, Improve, and Control.

Key Elements and Roles

Within the Six Sigma methodology, all matters go around three key elements, namely customers, processes, and employees. First, customers are the most important people to listen to. They give you more insights in terms of quality and other expectations. Customers are filled with expectations when they buy a product or service. Just think about it, if you order a physical product online, what things do you consider important? These are probably things like reliability, good prices, fast delivery, excellent service, et cetera. As an organization, you have to define and deliver these metrics to a high standard for the ultimate customer experience and, consequently, better customer satisfaction.

SecondF, an organization is nothing without its processes. Therefore, with Six Sigma, we spend a great deal of time defining processes, their metrics, and how we can adequately measure them because without measuring, we've no clue how matters are going. The processes aren't defined in a vacuum. Instead, these are represented by receiving customer feedback and looking at the processes from the customer's perspective.

Third, no process can run adequately without employees. If you wish to apply Six Sigma, all employees have to be on board and need to be involved. Of course, there's a clear learning curve involved in all this. To ease the learning, organizations can hold training sessions to instill key concepts further. Thereby, every employee should be able to use her/his skills to fulfill customer demands as well as possible. To properly get the ball rolling, the organization needs to take out some time to properly define roles and related objectives. Without doing the same, it's impossible to implement a robust Six Sigma methodology to satisfy your customer, because employees would, for instance, do tasks they are less suited for than a colleague.

Properly defining roles is crucial. All employees that are going to work with Six Sigma have a set of tasks to fulfill. In short, there are seven distinct sets of responsibilities. The first is the *leadership team*. This team is focused on getting all objectives defined properly for adequate Six Sigma processes. It can be compared to a Board in a corporate firm. Just as the Board defines a path, the same is done by the leadership team so that the employees meet the objectives they set. The leadership team has various responsibilities, such as: setting strict planning with deadlines of when specific work has to be completed, continuously explain how customer desires can be met even better, and supporting team members to grow their skills. The second is *the sponsor*. The so-called Six Sigma sponsor is knowledgeable about the process and is readily aiming for the most significant successes. Every Six Sigma project needs at least one sponsor to function properly. Usually, the sponsor is an executive of some sort and is readily focused on solving complex problems that pop up during the project. Besides, sponsors can be seen as owners too. They may not be the owners of the organization, but owners of processes instead. Improving and coordinating these processes is necessary for any good gains.

The third and fourth are the *implementation leader* or *champion* and *team leader*. The first has the responsibility of directing and motivating the employees who are part of the Six Sigma team. Besides, she/he supports the leadership team by communicating the completed work and possible obstacles the Six Sigma team faces. The second, team leader, has a more hands-on approach when dealing with the employees of the Six Sigma team. She/he communicates with the sponsor and makes sure the day to day tasks are fulfilled according to schedule. This schedule doesn't come falling from the sky. The schedule is created by the fifth role, namely the *coach*. The coach is a Six Sigma professional with the necessary certificates. She/he crafts the schedule defines tasks, and intermediates when conflicts arise. The sixth and seventh roles are as a *team member* and *process owner*. The team members are employees who work **in** the Six Sigma project itself instead of **on** it. The team member has deadlines to finish the stipulated work and communicates with other team members and the team leader. Finally, the process owner has the duty of ensuring that a process is fit for purpose. Usually, the responsibility of a process owner includes financing, design, change management, and continuous improvement of the process and associated measured values.

Process improvement is a challenge. If the right people with the right Six Sigma skills are involved, a significant and lasting change can be achieved. To define levels of expertise of the aforementioned organizational roles, every person involved in a Six Sigma project has a "belt color," as we see in martial arts. There are five important colored belts, namely:

> • First, the Yellow Belt. Employees with this belt understand the basic principles of Six Sigma. They pass on process problems to colleagues with Green and Black Belts. Also,

they participate in project teams and receive JIT (just-in-time) training.

• Second, the Orange Belt. These employees can apply the basic principles of Six Sigma practically. They have the possibility to manage small improvement projects.

• Third, the Green Belt. It starts and manages Six Sigma projects. Has Six Sigma expertise, but know fewer intricacies than people with Black Belts. Also, they give JIT (just-in-time) training to others.

• Fourth, the Black Belt. These employees report directly to a Master Black Belt. They have advanced expertise in Six Sigma. Additionally, they act as a coach, mentor, teacher, and project leader for project teams.

• Fifth, the Master Black Belt. This expert collaborates with leaders to identify gaps in projects and selects projects for improving processes. She/he provides coaching, mentorship, acts as a teacher, and leads projects independently. This expert is responsible for Six Sigma implementation and instilling a great culture in an organization.

Getting Started: The Steps and Tools

Before you can get started with Six Sigma, figure out if it's the right thing for your organization. For especially older, more static companies, change can be a tremendous challenge. Therefore, answer the below questions to get a better view of where your organization is standing at the moment:

• Would you say that the organization's strategic trajectory is clear?

• Would you say that the organization is efficient and effective when handling new situations?

• Has the organization evaluated the effectiveness of operation; how well are processes going?

- Can you make the needed investments (such as for training and consultation) and most probably lose in the short-term in order to win in the long-term?
- Are other aspects of the organization changing that are related to Six Sigma?

There are many more questions you could ask, but these are the most important ones, and answering these questions with Six Sigma experts should help you in making a readiness assessment to continue the effort or not.

If your organization decides to move forward, it has to draw out a path to achieve a Six Sigma organization. This is followed up by properly defining objectives, making these realistic and feasible, and gathering the necessary professionals. Afterward, the organization can immerse itself in creating the Six Sigma organization they desire by training its people and running a pilot Six Sigma project to test things out. The project could be assigned top-down or bottom-up. Both approaches have their up- and downsides. The first is heavily related to the strategy and customer needs, but the scope may be too wide. The latter has a small scope, but may not be very much related to the strategy. Six Sigma experts need to figure out a way between these two extremes to achieve the best results. As explained earlier, a Six Sigma project follows a couple of steps, namely Define, Measure, Analyze, Improve, and Control, which corresponds with the acronym DMAIC. Besides this method, there's another one with the acronym DMADV, which stands for Define, Measure, Analyze, Design, Verify. This book will expand on the first and most well-known method, DMAIC. The DMAIC cycle is a structured and proven method within Six Sigma to achieve better business results. Each phase within the DMAIC cycle contains useful tools and techniques that will guide you to achieve the defined organizational objectives.

DMAIC is a project-based and customer-centric approach to a problem, in which the causes and the solutions are still unknown. Thus, a project tackled through the DMAIC phases has a definite start and end. Because the client's wishes are dynamic, various DMAIC projects follow each other up (changing customer wishes lead to new challenges), making room for a culture where life-long learning and continuous improvement are first and foremost. Let's take a quick look through all the fact-based phases before we delve into any intricacies.

- **Define Phase – What's the problem at hand?** The problem is defined in this phase. This is done by answering the following questions:
    - What's the problem?
    - What's the scope?
    - Which customer segment is affected by the problem?
    - What would the business case look like?
    - What is planning, and what are the critical phases in the process?

Attention is also given in this phase to the soft side of change. Think of things like how to select the ideal project team, who are the stakeholders, and how can I influence them. At the end of the Define Phase, both the project manager and the client have a robust view of what the problem is.

Tools and techniques that are often used in this phase include The Process Map, Voice of the Customer (VoC), and SIPOC (Supplier, Input, Process, Output, Customer).

- **Measure Phase – How big is the problem at hand?** If all is done correctly, after the first phase, we end up with a clear problem statement. Afterward, the relevant data is measured and collected in the Measure Phase. The following questions require consideration:
    - How do we make sure that the information we gather is correct?
    - What's the size of the problem?

> o What information do I need, and what can I categorize?
> o How specific must it be, and how will I collect the information?

The Measure Phase validates the business case that was illustrated in the Define Phase. With tools such as the Pareto Chart, Trend Chart, and Detailed Process Map, it's possible to sharpen the scope further. If the scope is well-defined, we continue with the next phase.

> • **Analyze Phase – What are the root causes of the problem?** After the data has been collected and measured, it's analyzed in this phase. This includes attempting to recognize cause-effect relationships. Furthermore, the following answers are sought in this phase:
> o What is causing the problem?
> o What is the root cause of the problem?
> o Is further research needed? If so, what priorities do we set?

The Analysis phase approaches the possible causes from two sides, namely the data side and the process side. The process is analyzed to find out what regularly goes wrong, what adds value, and what doesn't. The data is used to substantiate the assumptions so that it's clear to everyone that the defined causes are indeed the root causes. To achieve this, we can use various tools and techniques such as The Histogram, 5-Why Analysis, and Regression Analysis.

> • **Improve Phase – What countermeasures do we implement?** Once the root causes are known, it is time to figure out improvements, test them, and implement them. For this phase, consider the following:
> o Know that the focal point remains on the best solutions. These solutions have a high probability of success and cost the least amount of resources.

o Ensure that the solutions are tested in a pilot. If the solution is tested successfully, it can be implemented in the real organization.

The most challenging aspect of this phase is the possible resistance the project leader will face for implementing the countermeasures. Therefore, in this phase, extra attention is given to resistance tools and techniques like brainstorming, Poka Yoke, and Deployment Flowchart.

- **Control Phase – How do we safeguard the countermeasures?** This phase is dedicated to safeguarding to prevent failure. The English verb "to control" in this context means "to manage." Related questions in this phase are:
  o How can I ensure adequate results and prevent failure?
  o How are we going to respond to signs of failure?
  o How can I visualize developments and identify trends early?

A successful project stands or falls by an excellent guarantee. If insufficient attention is paid to this, you may win in the short term, but will be very disappointed in the long term, because of the lack of competent assurance mechanisms.

In the coming chapters, all these phases and their essential tools and techniques will be addressed in more detail.

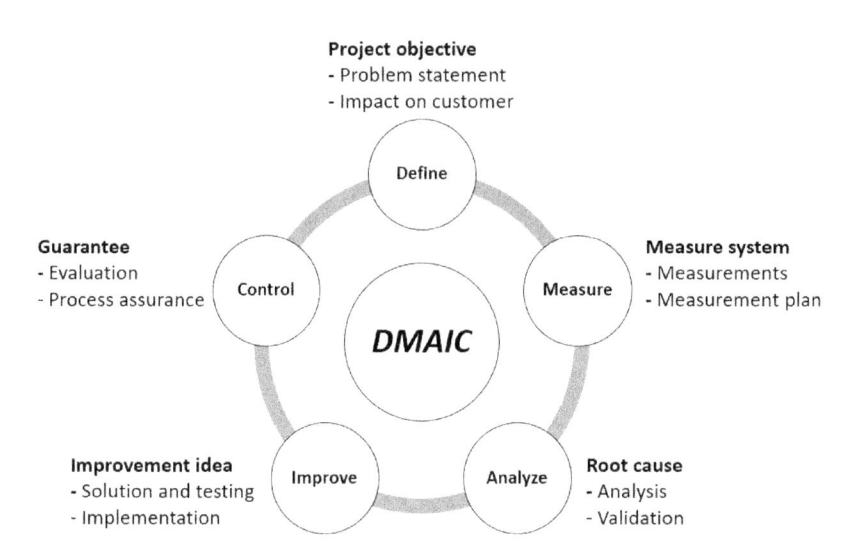

Image of the DMAIC Cycle. Define – Project objective, problem statement, impact on the customer: measure – Measure system, measurements, measurement plan. Analyze – Root cause, analysis, validation. Improve – Improvement idea, solution, and testing, implementation: control – Guarantee, evaluation, process assurance.

Chapter 3. Lean + Six Sigma = Lean Six Sigma

The first chapters were dedicated to two methodologies, namely Lean and Six Sigma. But what happens if we combine both these great methodologies? Well, Lean + Six Sigma = Lean Six Sigma. This is a new methodology that combines all benefits found within these two approaches of managing customers, projects, and processes. Lean Six Sigma is a globally proven methodology to attain sustainable forms of improvement of processes and organizations. The methodology proffers an approach by which organizations can achieve concrete results with continuous improvement in a structured manner (Define, Measure, Analysis, Improve and Control, or DMAIC). The focal point is on what customers find important and to realize this in processes. No more and no less. With this approach, costs are reduced, customer satisfaction is increased, and the lead time is shortened. The strength of this approach is that we make use of existing knowledge and experience of people within the processes. From the Lean Six Sigma methodology, both the process and the quality improve. Lean strives for more flow and value generation. Six Sigma strives for stable and effective processes. In combination, they reinforce each other and are entirely complimentary. Lean is for waste elimination and Six Sigma to reduce variation. Do you remember more about what you read about these methodologies? No worries if you don't remember much. Here are the key points to reinforce the ideas in your mind.

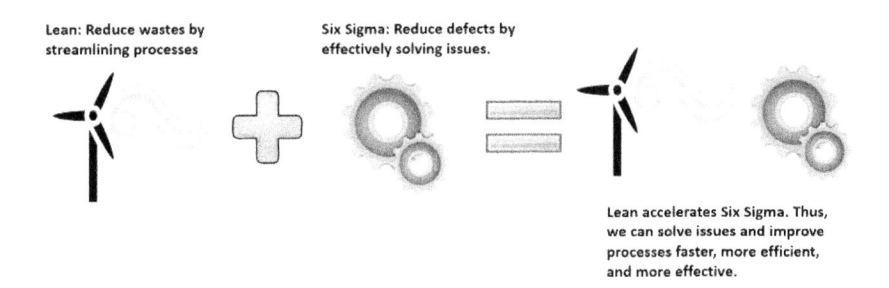

Image of a windmill with the text: "Lean: Reduce wastes by streamlining processes," an addition sign, an image if gear with the text: "Six Sigma: Reduce defects by effectively solving issues." Combine these images, and we get the following text: "Lean accelerates Six Sigma. Thus, we can solve issues and improve processes faster, more efficient, and more effective."

The basics of Lean can be deduced from the Toyota Production Systems (TPS). The Japanese inventor Taiichi Ohno is the founder of this system and based it on developments from other inventors such as Henry Ford and methodologies such as Business Process Redesign.

- Lean starts by determining the added value for the customer, a product, or service that meets certain conditions or specifications.

- The process that delivers this value is then mapped the so-called value flow.

- By carrying out this exercise, it becomes clear where waste is located, and an improved flow process can be made. These wastes become apparent through the collection of data around them, and together with the employees working in and on the process, it gets better step by step.

- Then, you look at how you can set up the process so that it starts when the customer requests it and then delivers precisely on time when the customer wants it.

- People in the organization see where improvements can be made and work on these. In this way, an organization is created in which there is a process-wide approach, and everything is focused on doing what the customer demands in a smart, effective, and efficient way.

Regarding Six Sigma, it was developed around the same time as Lean - and is more data-driven. The methodology has been developed by Motorola and has been widely and successfully applied by General Electric and many other organizations, small and big. The structured project approach Define, Measure, Analysis, Improve, and Control (DMAIC) ensures that the root cause of a problem is first found before a solution is implemented. By applying the DMAIC Model, you use the capacities of your employees within the organization structure efficiently and intelligently to create as much value as possible for the customer. A variant of this model is the DMADV: Define, Measure, Analyze, Design, and Verify or DFSS: Design For Six Sigma. By determining and measuring the critical indicators of the company, it becomes clear where improvements need to be made. The management receives targets and tools for this through Six Sigma, thus creating a structured improvement model. As with Lean, this is based on the added value for the customer.

There are many benefits to implementing both methods in the form of one way, i.e., Lean Six Sigma. Think of the following benefits:

- Lean Six Sigma increases the productivity and profit of your organization by improving the efficiency of your processes. Efficient processes result in products and services that are completed faster, without compromising on quality.

- Furthermore, Lean Six Sigma reduces costs for your organization by eliminating all activities that contribute nothing to the creation of products or services. By removing all these unnecessary activities in your processes, you also reduce complexity and improve communication in both your company and with your customers.

- Besides the application for specific improvement projects, Lean Six Sigma is very important for managing processes organization-wide. It provides a framework for reducing product defects, improving returns, limiting warranty costs, and improving delivery quality.

- Lean Six Sigma helps you change your organizational culture so that people have a similar understanding of doing business. This helps to guarantee the quality of your products and services. Your company changes from a reactive to a proactive organization that focuses on continuously satisfying customers, be they internal or external.'

Lean is focused on fast and efficient business processes, whereby quality assurance often turns out to be an issue. It does not matter how many forms have been filled or documents created if the stored information does not meet the requirements. Quickly completing activities without quality assurance leads to an environment that is error-prone, resulting in redoing the work. This is where Six Sigma becomes an essential part of process management. The Six Sigma methodology is a quality tool that emphasizes the reduction of errors in a process. It focuses on identifying variation in those factors that influence the result and looks for the real cause of errors with a Root Cause Analysis. Nowadays, Six Sigma plays a vital role in the leadership of an organization. Large-scale implementation can help a company achieve real and measurable results. From a distance, the two methods almost seem to be opposites. However, many practitioners argue that the best approach to achieving an effective and efficient business structure is to implement both Lean and Six Sigma. Besides, if a company opts for this combined implementation by two specialist practitioners, this can lead to a corporate culture where *thinkers* (Six Sigma) and *doers* (Lean) combine forces.

Both forces need to receive the correct training, so let's look at the possibilities for training and certifications in the next chapter.

Chapter 4. Training and Certifications: What Do I Need?

There are various ways to garner the necessary skills to conduct projects with Lean Six Sigma. Just like the Lean Six Sigma efforts themselves, the training programs vary from organization to organization. However, in practice, we tend to see various similar elements when training employees.

First, when an organization is entirely oblivious to Lean Six Sigma, it's best to start with an awareness course, i.e., White Belt training. The White Belt training gives a great overview and teaches the basics of Lean Six Sigma in a few hours. The aim is to introduce people to the language and concepts of Lean Six Sigma. Working on a project is usually not a condition.

Second, the organization can take up a more in-depth introductory course in the Yellow or Green Belt training programs. This next-level includes a direction in which people can practice using the improvement methods and tools. In larger organizations, this training can take up to one to two weeks. The Yellow Belt is an intermediate step between the White Belt and the Green Belt. The training of a Yellow Belt is usually a bit shorter than that of a Green Belt. If employees want to become a Green Belt, they are usually expected to be able to manage projects. If someone wants to become a Yellow Belt, she/he only needs to participate in a project but doesn't have to lead it.

Third, the organization can focus on training a few professionals to become especially skilled in all facets of Lean Six Sigma, with the Black Belt Training. The Black Belts form the core of the Lean Six Sigma support structure. In some companies, they manage projects; in other companies, they work as coaches on different projects simultaneously. Fourth, for an elite group of professionals, it's possible to go even further, with a Master Black Belt training. This training consists of a handful of refined Lean Six Sigma tools. Not every Black Belt needs to learn these techniques because they are not as common as the general Lean Six Sigma instruments. These skills are often offered as part of the training for a Master Black Belt or in specialized in-depth courses for Black Belts. A full Black Belt training usually takes four to six weeks, one of which focuses on leadership training. Typically, the Black Belts follow one week of training, then they work on a project for a couple of weeks, return for training a couple of days and get back in the trenches. It's a very hands-on approach to learning.

The training consists of Lean and Six Sigma methods, "complexity reduction" methods, as well as project management and leadership skills. Each participant receives one to five days of support from a Master Black Belt with experience in implementing improvements and managing projects from different sizes and organizations. In terms of forms, training can be followed through online courses or can be conducted in person, for instance, by hiring a Master Black Belt consultant in house. With many courses available today, participants have access to both electronic and printed training materials, case studies, and other resources.

For each of the belts mentioned above, it's possible to get certified. For most organizations, it's not needed to acquire a certification. Having the basic knowledge of Lean Six Sigma can be acquired through other sources too, such as the book you're reading now. Properly going through this book will give you more than enough knowledge to get going with Lean Six Sigma without any additional training. However, if you would like to acquire a certification (perhaps your ideal job requires this), pay attention to a few things. When you attempt to get certified, always make sure the training organization is appropriately recognized and legitimate. For instance, The International Association for Six Sigma Certification (IASSC) delivers training programs and accredited certifications upon completion of exams.

Chapter 5. The Lean Six Sigma Process: DMAIC VS DMADV

Now that we have a good overview of Lean, Six Sigma, and Lean Six Sigma, it's time to focus on the practical side of Lean Six Sigma. In this chapter, we take a closer look at the Lean Six Sigma process and how you can implement the same.

As explained previously in this book, there are two critical methodologies for implementing Lean Six Sigma in your organization, namely DMAIC and DMADV. In this chapter, you'll learn more about both these natural processes and their benefits, so that you can decide the process you'd like to follow.

DMAIC

So, what is DMAIC about? As explained in a previous chapter, it consists of five phases that seamlessly merge into a cycle process and is an acronym for Define, Measure, Analyze, Improve, and Control. Let's take a look at each phase:

- **Define.** The problem is defined in this first phase. In addition, it is important to recognize and define the following components:
  - What is the goal, and what are the related business processes?
  - Who are the customers?

o What are the critical phases in the process?
- **Measure.** In this phase, the most important aspects of the current process are measured, and relevant data is collected. The following points are essential:
  o Analysis of input and output.
  o Definition of the measurement plan.
  o Testing of the measuring system.
- **Analysis.** Subsequently, the investigated data is analyzed. We look at the different cause-effect relationships. The root cause of defects and errors is sought out. Essential tools and techniques are used to:
  o Detect gaps between the current performance and the desired performance.
  o Identify the input and the output.
  o Prioritizing potential opportunities.
- **Improve.** The current process is improved in this phase with the help of techniques and creative solutions. Brainstorming sessions can be a useful tool. Other apparent solutions are:
  o Innovative ideas.
  o Focus on the simplest and most comfortable solutions.
  o Prepare a detailed implementation plan.
  o Implementation of improvements via, for example, a quality circle.
  o Finding out errors and causes, using an Ishikawa diagram.
- **Control.** This phase is not just about control, and it's more about supervision.
  o Control takes care that any possible defects in the future are prevented as much as possible. Supervision leads to lasting improvement and therefore guarantees long-term success.

In addition to the standard DMAIC model, it's wise to also implement this step-by-step plan in other business processes. By sharing experience and newly acquired knowledge with other departments, changes can be made more efficiently throughout the entire organization. It's essential that employees have a good understanding of the usefulness of the working method of the DMAIC model, that they can discuss this well with each other, and are willing to share experiences. The DMAIC model was initially linked to Six Sigma and is intended to improve the quality of the production (output) of a process. This is done by identifying and removing the causes of errors. However, the DMAIC model is not exclusive to Six Sigma and can, therefore, be used to improve processes at other organizations.

Furthermore, The DMAIC model is an application of the PDCA cycle of William Edwards Deming. Where the DMAIC model is based more on a project-based approach to the problem, the PDCA cycle is both widely applicable and applicable to one project. The DMAIC model analyzes the root cause of the problem, while the PDCA cycle focuses attention on the whole and also uncovers other causes. Besides, the DMAIC model is based on framework thinking within, for example, product group, customer group, or service department. The strength of the model lies in tackling and optimizing root causes of problems in a process. However, the model is less applicable for a completely creative change in which the course within an organization is completely reversed. When going through the steps in the DMAIC model, there should not be any overlap. The best results are achieved with a planned team approach.

To further illustrate this, take the steel manufacturer NewSteel I just came up with. NewSteel has 20 locations nationwide and is specialized in car frames. Until now, they have plenty of stock of various types of frames in every branch. This allows them to help the customer quickly. This subsequently results in satisfaction and good word-of-mouth advertising. Now it appears that last year the costs of the steel manufacturer have increased rapidly. Therefore, the management decides to enter into a dialogue with all 20 location leaders and find out what could be the cause, by using DMAIC.

- **Define.** The costs have gone up considerably and include personnel costs, renting the 20 properties and inventory.
- **Measure.** The costs are compared with the norm of the previous year, and it appears that the costs are 20% higher, without more turnover being generated.
- **Analysis.** In consultation with all 20 supervisors, the largest cost item was examined. This reveals various factors. On average, it appears that the inventory costs at all locations were 15% higher than the year before, which is partly due to too little variety, which means that "older" models of frames remain in the warehouse longer.
- **Improve.** Together with the 20 branch location leaders, the management is looking for possible improvements. For example, the proposal is to work with a central warehouse, from which the locations will be supplied two to three times a week. Another possibility is to only stock standard frames and to store the more specific types of frames in the central warehouse. After a discussion with the NewSteel supervisors, they selected the first solution.
- **Control.** After a test period, an evaluation takes place with all supervisors and the management. It appears that NewSteel often has to sell "no" to the customers or that customers can only be helped with a delay of several days. After this evaluation, they considered the second solution they had at their disposal and decided to have the most commonly used frames in stock per location. Also, they decided to deliver the remaining frames from the central warehouse. Of course, a test period and evaluation will take place after this choice, and the costs are also passed on.

DMADV

Now, what is DMADV about? DMADV stands for:

- **D**efine
- **M**easure
- **A**nalyze
- **D**esign
- **V**erify

It is a quality method used for designing new processes to ensure that, when the end-product goes to the customer, it is delivered correctly. The method's purpose is to create the highest quality products, keeping the end-customer and their needs in mind throughout each of the five phases listed above.

With Six Sigma, the efforts are related to process improvement within quality management. Existing products and/or services are improved through analytical techniques and statistics. Six Sigma focuses on reducing variation in issues that are perceived as Critical to Quality (CTQ) by the customer. These CTQs are very important and crucial for quality; it concerns the internal critical quality parameters that relate to the wishes and needs of the customer. CTQs are, therefore, quality properties of the process or service that meet what the customer considers important.

The DMADV model revolves around the development of a new service, product, or process. The DMADV model is especially useful when implementing new strategies and initiatives. Consider the following phases:

- **Define.** This first phase of the DMADV model is about identifying the purpose of the project, process, or service. Not only seen from the perspective of the organization but also from the perspective of stakeholders, including internal and external customers. It must be clearly defined which guidelines are essential for the development of a product or service, whether there are potential risks and what the production planning is. During this first phase, the project leader finds out the customer's most important requirements as far as the service or product being developed is concerned. How? By using customer information relevant to the project and feedback from the customer. As an example, look at a company called GardenJoy. They make garden furniture, and, in the first phase, they may opt to focus solely on garden benches constructed of wood. Because of the information they obtained from the customer earlier, they know that the customer wants fair trade wood used. As well, the customer has said the benches must be big enough for a minimum of two people, the headrest and backrest must be comfortable, and the coating must be environmentally friendly; that way, they can leave the furniture outdoors all year round. In this first phase, the manufacturer will also consider whether a bench such as this would be profitable to develop.

- **Measure.** The second phase is focused on the collection/recording of data relevant to the measures (CTQ) that the first phase identified. This data is critical as it drives the entire process. In the DMADV Measurement phase, CTQs do not exist. Why? Because their product hasn't been manufactured so we can't even begin to examine the production process. Instead, we look at exactly what the customer requires; these factors then get linked to the quality, and the CTQs are then created. If every design component is assigned a value, it follows that a practical approach should be created for getting the production process off the ground.

Now is when it is critical to determine the production parts important to all the stakeholders. Ultimately, the customers' needs will be turned into clear objectives, ensuring a product that stands apart from its competitors is created. GardenJoy now takes the important customer requirements and links to them to the CTQs. If fair trade wood cannot be procured, the production will not go ahead. That also applies to the coating – if it isn't environmentally friendly, it can't happen. And lastly, the design – if the requirements of at least two spaces, a comfortable headrest and backrest cannot be met, the production will not begin. In this phase, the manufacturer will also look at the costs of production, design, and materials to see if they are more or less than the final price.

- **Analyze.** This DMADV phase goes together with the previous phase; at the time the data is collected, the project team must also analyze it. With this, we get the best basis for improvement measurements during production. It is also in this phase that the alternative designs are developed, and all the different requirement combinations are looked at. Here, an estimate is produced of the total costs of the entire design process and, once all the design alternatives have been considered, a rough design I the product is made, meeting the CTQs as near as possible.

Here, GardenJoy examines all the potential importers for fair trade timber, looking at where the wood originates so the information can go in the sales report. They look at the different coatings, working out the pros and cons of the environmentally friendly ones, as well as looking at the quality.

This is one of the most time-consuming phases because, on top of all that, the team must also analyze all the different designs. Here, the manufacturer would benefit from having a deadline in place; otherwise, the costs could spiral out of control.

- **Design.** In this phase, the product or service design is drawn up to the customer's requirements. The project team takes all the previous data and ensures that the product or service is suitable and that all the adjustments that can be made are. The design is incredibly detailed and of high quality, working as a prototype and includes consideration for the production process. The idea is not just coming up with the process to manufacture the right goods; it must also be an efficient process, in all areas. GardenJoy has considered their analysis and made their decisions – they have a fair-trade wood supplier; they know which of the environmentally friendly coatings to use, the design includes a safe, comfortable adjustment, and the right seat back and headrests. With manufacturing, one of the critical considerations must be how the machinery is laid out to ensure the process is fast, safe, and efficient in that the highest possible number of benches may leave the factory.

- **Verify.** This may be the final phase, but it certainly isn't where the process ends. For the quality to be guaranteed, the product must be continually checked and adjusted where needed. The design is completed, and the product may now be sold. During the Verify phase, the customer provides the team with feedback on the product and their experience; this is used to tweak the product to ensure it meets the exact requirements of the customer. The team also forms extra CTQ measures, so the feedback can be followed once the product has been delivered.

For GardenJoy, they must use this phase to see what the customer thinks. Is the fair trade wood good enough? Is the bench comfortable? Easy to use? Is the coating, right? And so on. If, after a month or two, they start to see negative reviews about the product, they know that something needs to be changed, and the data collected in previous phases is used to make those changes.

DMAIC VS DMADV

DMADV and DMAIC are similar; both are easily utilized with Lean Six Sigma and are identical in some ways. One of the most critical of these similarities is that they both aim to improve business processes, ensuring they are both effective and efficient. While the first three letters in each acronym are the same, they are not interchangeable and are, in fact, each used for a different purpose.

The primary difference is in the final two steps of each model; DMAIC focuses on improvement and control of the existing process while DMADV focuses on the development of new service/products.

As such, it is in the second model, where the customer requirements are emphasized. When a new service or product is developed, it must include everything the customer requires- and at the best of quality. Product designs meeting the criteria are known as DfSS, or "Designed for Six Sigma." More often than not, there may be a third criterion to DMADV – logistically, the production process has to be highly efficient. Then, we can talk in terms of DfLSS – "Designed for Lean Six Sigma."

Additionally, DMAIC carries out interim checks, improving the process where needed and reducing or eliminating defects. With DMADV, the focus is on the development of suitable models that fully meet the requirements of the customer, as we saw in the GardenJoy example. While the DMAIC cycle focuses on eliminating sub-standard quality, the DMADV cycle focuses on developing new quality features. This difference is amplified, especially in the Measure phase. At DMAIC, Critical to Quality (CTQ) parameters are measured that are most frequently outside the specifications. Afterward, the causes are identified and noted.

On the contrary, with DMADV, there are no CTQs at all in the measure phase. After all, there is no new product yet, let alone a production process! In this case, the measure phase includes determining what the customer considers important for a new product. The goal is to arrive at a Design Scorecard. This Scorecard contains the characteristics that the product must have to be useful in the market. In short, the Measure phase ultimately yields new CTQs. The Scorecard is used in the remainder of the product development process to check whether the design has these features.

All in all, both approaches DMAIC and DMADV can be used in specific contexts. It's up to you as a project manager to select the corresponding method. Are you willing to improve an existing business process? Then DMAIC is the way to go. Are you ready to (re)design a new product or service? Then DMADV is the way to go. Because this book is more about dealing with existing processes with the help of Lean Six Sigma, we'll delve deeper into the DMAIC approach. Let's get this going!

Chapter 6. Define: Process Mapping and Customer Voice

Every larger organization knows the situation that a problem seems to be solved, and yet it reappears day after day. The whole organization works hard, sometimes for months on end, to fix the issue. Now it will finally be solved, is what goes through the minds, but again things go wrong. An organization that works with Lean Six Sigma cannot afford such failures and therefore uses a more robust and dynamic solution method, namely DMAIC. DMAIC has proven to be one of the most effective problem-solving methods. Teams are forced to work with data. Data is important to achieve goals, such as finding the root cause of a problem and what processes the problem is related to. In this chapter, we take a look at the first phase, namely the *Define Phase*.

What is the Define Phase?

The Define Phase is the phase where the problem is identified. The purpose of this first phase in the DMAIC process is that all members of the team and the sponsors agree on what the project entails. There are a few activities to undertake in this phase:

- Search and gather data about customers for customers.
- Check the existing data about the process and/or the problem.
- Ensure that the entire team is involved in the project charter, a key element in planning a Lean Six Sigma project.
- You outline the improvement process in the outline. This type of process overview is a widely used improvement tool in DMAIC. In the "Define phase" of the DMAIC process, they are used to indicate the limits of the project.
- Prepare a plan and write guidelines for your team.

Besides these activities, consider these matters that follow, below.

These activities help you to clear up misunderstandings about the how and why of the project. Everyone employee on the team must be on the same line. A team often gets stuck as soon as there is disagreement about which data has to be collected or which solution is the best. Such a situation can occur if employees do not realize that they have different views on the project and the objective.

Talk to your customers and study the data that you have available. This is essential because then you know for sure whether the solutions also have a chance of success. It helps you to refine the goals of the project further. In exceptional cases, a project can be canceled if the data shows that it is not useful to continue working.

Come to an agreement with the management about a realistic scope of the project. If your team believes that the project is too large or too small, consult with management about possible changes. For example, you can add resources or adjust the deadline.

Make clear agreements about the standards for measuring success. A common mistake is that teams and stakeholders have not determined in advance when the project can be called successful. For example, a team is satisfied because it sees the number of errors decrease, but the only thing the manager wanted was an increase in sales. A team needs to know exactly what a sponsor pays attention to when assessing the result.

The All-Star LSS Team is formed and gathered to achieve worthwhile success. A team can consist of employees who already work together daily, but also of people from different departments. So it may be that the team members do not know each other. At this stage of the process, they have the opportunity to get to know each other.

Process Mapping: SIPOC

A core principle of Lean Six Sigma is that a defect can be anything that makes a customer unsatisfied, whether this is long delivery time, variation in the delivery time, poor quality, or high costs. To address these issues, be the first to look at the process in your company. To what extent does your company meet the specific wishes of the customer? What influences a process, and who has to deal with it? A SIPOC provides insight into this. It maps out the process that you want to improve and helps you determine the scope. It's an acronym for:

- **S**upplier
- **I**nput
- **P**rocess
- **O**utput
- **C**ustomer

The supplier provides the input for a process (step), and the output goes to the customer. The output must meet or exceed customer requirements.

There are many benefits to working with SIPOC. A SIPOC model can provide some insight into possible areas for improvement that can be explored further in a later stage. Above all, the purpose of a SIPOC is to define the boundaries of a project (scoping) by displaying a clear start and endpoint and ensuring that the process is divided into 5 to 7 well-arranged process steps. Another benefit is that this tool adds visualization to the conversation about the process. This helps the team members to gain a lot of value that would otherwise be lost in translation by only speaking without visualizing. It structures the conversation you are having and facilitates the discussion about the process. In addition, you acquire a good view of the customer and other stakeholders. Ignoring important stakeholders damages the relationship, and it will cost you time and energy later in the project to restore this. And above all: because it teaches you as a project manager to quickly come to the essence of the problem and process!

How does this look like in practice? In the first conversations with the stakeholders, you ask the customer to tell more about the process that needs improvement. You do this based on the following steps:

- Draw the structure of the SIPOC on a flip chart or whiteboard and grab some post-its with you.
- Determine the input? This can, for example, involve a telephone call from a customer, a delivery of raw materials, or a complaint. It is often a noun.
- Who supplies this input? (this is the Supplier!)
- What is the first thing that happens with the input? (that will be the first step in SIPOC, registration here)

You then work out the successive steps until you reach a concrete result:

- What is the result (which output)?
- Who receives this output?
- The recipient of the output is the customer of our process. This "customer" sets requirements for the output, for example, when it comes to quality (good solution in terms of content), but also to timeliness (within which period?), or to the method of delivery (personal, e-mail, social media, et cetera).
- And then, what requirements does 'the process' make of the input? This is very important because if your inputs are bad, your outputs will be bad too. Remember garbage in, garbage

out! Therefore, the input must also be of good quality to be properly processed.

With the SIPOC model, we can see which department delivers what part of the production and what the result is. It is also much clearer who the customer is. Below, you can see the SIPOC model elements are, explained using a real-world example:

- **Supplier** – the person/people who contribute to the entire process; they may be internal to the organization or external. We answer the question of what is required and used for the process in the next point, but this one is about who supplies the input. This is the party that supplies everything needed for the process, be it raw materials, information, skills, or knowledge. Going back to GardenJoy, they need several different suppliers to produce a garden bench. They need materials, designers, software suppliers, specialists, and employees. All of those are suppliers because they each supply something for the manufacturing process – raw materials, drawing and design software, designers, specialist employees, and so on.
- **Input** – now they have the suppliers, it is much easier to work out what is delivered, and that means you can work out what the inputs are. The input section is all about the service, materials, and information required by one or more of the process steps. What is required for a step? GardenJoy requires raw materials in the form of wood; they need glue, nails, and handles, and the software must be applied correctly. On top of that, they need the right tools and machines to do the job.
- **Process** – this is a series of steps that make sure the input gets converted into the right output – the service or product. Typically, a manual, documents, or set of instructions is used to record this; provided each step is described properly, the output will be correctly delivered with few to no deviations. Back to GardenJoy, by doing this, they can ensure that their

product leaves the manufacturing plant in bulk, barely differing from one another and all of the exact same quality. GardenJoy has a simple process – draw up the design, bring in the materials, construct the garden bench, package, and ship it to the relevant customer.

- **Output** – this is all about the end result, be it a service, a product, or information going to the customer. It covers what the steps deliver and what the customer requires for the end-product. Another part of the output that must be considered is waste – for GardenJoy, think of the bench as the end product and things like wood splinters as wastes.

- **Customer: Who are the customers?** This is any party that receives output from the process. This can be organizations, people, departments, but also *systems.* Who is the output for? The person or thing that receives the product or service is the end-user or customer. That may be the actual customer who purchases furniture from the factory, but it can also be the employee who wants to buy furniture for her/his department. The customer requirements are important for the entire process. If the output does not meet the customer requirements, the quality cannot be guaranteed. GardenJoy focuses on selling Business to Consumers (B2C) and Business to Business (B2B).

The above shows that we only mention first-line suppliers and customers within the SIPOC model. This means that other stakeholders, such as banks, subsidy providers, or licensing authorities, cannot be found in the SIPOC model. Besides, it's not common for the quality properties and/or specifications to be displayed. Furthermore, it's crucial to craft a SIPOC diagram with a group of employees, allowing all stakeholders to contribute to the process. Doing this in a vacuum will result in much confusion and brings the process in danger. Employees can bring their insight to the table and determine their role within the process. A SIPOC model creates mutual understanding and a shared view of the process and the reason behind it, and this leads to a high degree of involvement. This prevents uncertainty in the later phase of the process.

Now that you know what the SIPOC diagram is all about, let's fill it in! The steps you should take to fill in the SIPOC diagram are the following:

- **First, print or draw a SIPOC diagram and give it a clear title.** If you want to draw it out, make sure there's enough room to write. Now that you have a SIPOC diagram in front of you, ensure you have a clear name for the process you want to map out. Put this above the diagram as a title.
- **Second, accurately define the starting and ending points of the process you want to improve.** Often, these can be found on the team charter in the "scope" section.
- **Third, jot down the remaining parts of the process, around 4-8 main steps.** Don't do more than eight steps, or the process becomes long-winded. Don't do less than four, or the process becomes poorly-defined. These are the raw and most critical steps in the process. They don't include any decision points or feedback loops.
- **Fourth, write down the most critical outputs of the process you're tackling.** In practice, we see that the list of outputs includes around three or four main items.
- **Fifth, adequately define who is going to receive these outputs: who are the customers?** Again, these customers can be internal or external, and it can be a person, organization, or even a system or machine.
- **Sixth, jot down the inputs needed for the process.** Like the outputs don't go overboard in mentioning every intricacy. We're not interested in knowing that a laptop and stapler was used to print a document and staple it.
- **Seventh, for the final step, define and list the actors who supply the inputs to the process.** Do you make use of manufacturers? Are there specific professionals in your organization needed to make the process work? These

questions help you define who supplies the inputs to the process.

Voice of the Customer: Identifying and Understanding Customers

The goal with the Voice of the Customer (VOC) is collecting and recording customer requirements/expectations for the process you want to tackle. We apply the VOC when problems/assignments are linked to the customer, and this is usually the case. Mapping requirements is essential: if you don't know what the requirements are, how can you know if a process is causing problems? You can't. Therefore, take the following steps:

- Discuss and align with the owner of the assignment or project. What does she/he want to achieve? The owner of the project can be the team leader, but also the CEO, depending on the size and culture of the organization.
- Interview employees who readily talk with customers, such as customer service representatives.
- Approach customers and talk to them. For the most part, having a relaxed conversation is advised, but also make room for some more in-depth interviews with a selected group of customers. Besides, it's possible to garner more information with a survey. There are many websites whereby you can do a survey and have it promoted to your ideal customers, such as SurveyMonkey.
- Record any customer requirements/expectations that come up. You can use a tool such as a Kano model for this. Afterward, possibly translate this into indicators and specific standards.

After having a clear image who the different customers or customer groups are, you can start defining the VOC using these points of advice:

- Before using any online questionnaire, try to collect information directly from the mouths of the customers, based on open questions. Use techniques like the "5x why?" Method (explained in a later chapter) to get to the heart of the wish. Clients reason from their existing frame of reference and are not always aware of the possibilities that a product or service has to offer.
- Organize a Customer Journey Mapping session, in which you go through your process from the customer's perspective. When do we have contact with the customer? And how does the customer experience our process?
- A mistake that many make is to think that mapping the Voice of the Customer is a *one-time* process; both customers - and their wishes - are continually changing because they change over time. This process is accelerated by the technological developments that we see all around us. Because the Voice of the Customer is continuously changing, as an organization, you will have to stay in constant contact with your customers.

How we make the VoC concrete is by attaching critical quality characteristics to the wishes of the customer. Within Lean and Six Sigma, we call this Critical To Quality (CTQ, more on this later). Once it's clear what our customers want, we can continue with the Kano model to place and prioritize these customer wishes, so that we can get to work with the Voice of the Customer in a structured way.

The success of a product or service is ultimately determined by what the customer thinks and says. Three types of properties influence customer perception and are easy to trace with the Kano model. This model for customer satisfaction is a useful tool to develop precisely those product characteristics that make the difference. The primary or expected properties are so obvious that the customers do not even mention them when asked. Although they don't mention these properties, they indeed assume that they're met. If that's not the case, great dissatisfaction is the result. Performance characteristics are things usually expressed by customers when asked what they expect from a product. If the product performs better, its satisfaction will increase; if it performs less, satisfaction will decrease. Attractive features make the customer say "WOW!" They are often unconscious wishes or hidden needs. If they're missing, the customer does not miss them, but if they are present, customer satisfaction increases exponentially.

Chapter 7. Measure: Project WHY's, Data, and Defects

Measuring is the process by which numbers and symbols are assigned to concepts or objects in reality. This is done in such a way and according to agreed rules so that it's evident for all employees. Measuring is essential for gaining an objective understanding of what is going on, and how big, small, heavy, light, how much or how little a matter is. Measuring is central to Six Sigma because it's used as a tool to learn how causal relationships are. Measuring helps to learn what parameters influence the final result. People in the process must be allowed to perform these measurements. Please note that a distinction is made between measurements of the process and measurements that are focused on the *outcome of the process.*

To further illustrate this, take Andrew Johnson, a college student who wants to gain more weight or muscle. After a consultation with his dietician, he found out that he weighs 132 pounds, but needs to weigh around 176 to match his height. Together they make a program to increase his weight to 176 pounds. They make an appointment every other week for a consultation. At the start of the meeting, Andrew must always stand on a scale, and not only his weight is measured, but also his muscle mass and fat percentage. These are the *result measurements* of his weight gain process; these results reflect the effect of the diet. But these measurements do not help with the weight gain process itself. After all, if you see no improvement (weight does not increase), you have no idea what's going on. That's why Andrew is instructed to keep a notebook in which he writes down how many calories he eats, how many exercise hours he does per day, and how high his heart rate is during these exercise hours. We call these *process measurements*. After all, this diet and life schedule is based on the knowledge that with proper exercise (weight training) and a more healthy calorie intake, Andrew will gain weight. This relationship between process and result can be checked in this way. At the same time, you will see that Andrew isn't going to structure his lifestyle based on weight, but according to his *process measurements*: calories and exercise. These are the parameters on which he has direct influence and which positively influence the ultimately desired result. Moreover, it gives the dietitian the possibility to check how Andrew's weight gaining process is progressing. The essence of measuring is that not only are results measured, but those process owners, in particular, do process measurements, and then specifically on those parameters that have a (proven) causal relationship with the result measurements.

What is the Measure Phase?

In the Measure phase, we determine what the measurement procedure is and how well the measurement system can measure the CTQs (Critical to Qualities). The team must ensure that the measurement system - and the data collected with it - is valid and reliable before continuing to analyze this data. To make a statement about this, a Measurement System Analysis (MSA) is performed on the measurement system. The Measure phase is often seen as the most challenging phase of a DMAIC project because reliable data is sometimes lacking, and it's challenging to implement an MSA. For Lean projects, it's critical to clearly define the definitions of the CTQ and the source for the data, so that there is no discussion about performance. The difference between the current performance (Baseline performance) and the desired performance is also determined within the Measure phase (Target performance).

Measuring is essential in Lean Six Sigma. Measuring can make or break your Lean Six Sigma project. If you don't collect any data, you will be confronted with disappointing results. Even if you win a little in the short term, the long run will catch on to you. The combination of data, knowledge, and experience is what ensures real improvement in a process. Measuring involves the following:

- You evaluate the existing measurement system and make improvements where necessary. If you do not yet have a measuring system, you need to develop or buy one.
- You collect data and observe the process.
- You map the process with more depth.

So, why is this necessary? You must be able to trust your data. It often happens that a team has spent a lot of time collecting data and then finding out that the measurement system used is unreliable. They discover, for example, that the clock was always switched on at different times in the process. As a result, they read a different turn-around time each time. Employees may misread an instrument or use different definitions of "defect." If you make your decisions depend on data, make sure that you can trust what the data tells you.

Furthermore, because DMAIC is a method based on data, you base decisions on facts and reality. People's opinions still count, but everything has to be balanced against what the data has to say to you. Also, you record what is really going on in a process so that employees know of each other what they're working on. Finally, you understand what needs to be improved and what doesn't. The key lies in what we have addressed earlier in this book, namely, out of the numerous activities your organization or department performs, only a handful of activities are of real importance to customers. It's your job to track down and improve these core activities. After that, you must eliminate as much work as possible without added value.

Data Types and Data Collection

In the Measure Phase, data is essential. Without data, the whole DMAIC model is useless. We distinguish two forms of data, namely qualitative or discrete data or quantitative or continuous (numerical) data. Both forms are used to collect data. Regarding qualitative data, proper measurements start by asking relevant questions, which means interviewing customers to work out what those questions are. By asking relevant questions, they can produce a rough prototype of a value model that has plenty of clarifying power; this, in turn, leads to the right decisions being made. The customers must be listened to when they talk about what they consider when they purchase a product or service from you. The primary focus should be on the customers in the relevant market segment. If you rely solely on your own internal judgments about the questions to ask, it will likely lead to weaker models and questionnaires that are just too long, and both of these are nothing more than a waste of time, money, and energy.

As far as qualitative research goes, this is about identifying what criteria are used by customers to evaluate their purchase options, looking at image, quality, and price. It is those criteria that the survey is based on, where customers are requested to rate how they felt your organization performed. This may be done over the phone, via the internet, or even in person, and that will depend on the size of the market and what products or services you offer.

There should be survey questions that verify the right person is answering the questions too. The survey scores are used in many different statistical tools for producing what is known as the Market Value Model. As such, the importance attached to image, quality, and price becomes fully visible during the value definition for the product and/or market; at the same time, the CTQ (Critical to Quality) factors are determined together with the importance of each. The result is a CTQ determination driven by data and facts that can, in turn, drive products, people, and improvements to the process through the entire organization.

Identifying Project Ys

Variation or spread is simply a deviation from the expectation. To further understand how to deal with data, I want to introduce a fundamental Six Sigma equation, namely: $Y = f(X) + \varepsilon$.

- First, we define "Y" as the result that you want to achieve.
- Second, we define "X" as the input. By the input or inputs, it's possible to get to the result.
- Third, we define "f" as the function. This is the manner with which your input transforms into the outcome.
- Fourth, we define "ε" (Greek letter epsilon) as the presence of defects or errors.

In simpler terms, the input is transformed by a process to the desired output.

To further illustrate this, take Amy, who wants to make cupcakes. She takes softened butter, eggs, self-rising flour, and the remaining ingredients necessary. Afterward, these ingredients are transformed by mixing and baking, to the desired outcome. The ingredients are the inputs (Xs), mixing, and baking is the function of the transformation process, and the resulting delicious cupcakes are the Y.

Not very hard math, right? Well, there's one more aspect, because, in practice, an outcome *always has a degree of uncertainty or variation*. It doesn't matter if the best chefs make the cupcakes or Amy makes the cupcakes; there's still some indefiniteness about the extent to which their actions produce the ideal outcome.

Just think about it. What if Amy didn't use enough softened butter or the oven wasn't set to the right temperature? Suppose Amy bake twenty cupcakes; would they all be ultimately the same? Nope, the cupcakes will- at least - differ slightly from each other. In Six Sigma, the small error that creeps in and causes this variation is represented by the "ε." These errors or defects can come from Amy herself (such as if she used the wrong temperature to bake the cupcakes), or be random (such as when the power goes out.) No matter the situation, there's always room for variation. So, let's take a closer look at it.

Variations and Defects

Variation or spread is simply a deviation from the expectation. To better understand variation, take Pablo, who flips a coin. How big is the chance that Pablo throws either heads or tails? If the coin is not spun, the likelihood is fifty percent. So when he tosses a coin twenty times, you expect ten times heads and ten times tails. Based on the probability, this is what we would expect. But is this true, or are we just assuming? Well, you can try it yourself; toss a coin ten times and see if you get five times heads and five times tails. Most likely, you won't. Why? Because there is *variation*, i.e., the output (the number of times head and coin) varies per series of ten flips. The degree to which your experience deviates from the expectation is the degree of variation.

When you accurately measure an output Y, you will see that it always varies no matter how hard we strive to make duplicates. Every output varies. Every single service or product that a business makes has differences in things like size, color, material, and degree of customer satisfaction. When you measure the event of something often, it will vary around the *average* value. Toss a coin often enough, and you see that the average of heads and tails tends to be around the 50/50 mark. When you measure the value of a given event, it will vary relative to the average. A top NBA player may have an average point per game of 29 over a whole season. However, in the game last Wednesday, he scored 25 points; this Wednesday, he scored 33 points - more than his average of 29. Why? These are examples of variation: the variation of the event relative to the average. The scope, trends, nature, causes, consequences, and control of this variation are the eternal obsession of Six Sigma. Nothing more is studied or treated than this in Six Sigma.

Measuring is the collection of data related to the input (the Xs) and the given outcome (the Y) that results from the process function "f". Measurements give you a quantitative understanding of the characteristics of the input and how this is related to the desired outcome. Measuring the input gives you a profile of the way a process runs concerning a goal or objective. Measuring starts with the Ys and then extends to the Xs to understand the causes. Let's make this more clear with an example. Mary, a college student, would love to have an extra $500 in her wallet, and this is her desired outcome Y. To measure her progress, Mary could check her purse every single day and count the number of dollar bills she has and finds she has too little compared to the ideal amount she wants. Mary could analyze the situation and conclude that the amount of money in her wallet is a function of how much she earns at her side job, how much taxes she pays, and how much she spends. These are the inputs (Xs). To have any form of influence, she needs to do something about the Xs mentioned to change Y. To bring about a change in the output Y, the person should measure and control the performance of the causal Xs. For instance, Mary could decide to find another side job to earn more or she could spend less money on buying things.

Unfortunately, most people never get past the Y. They look at it, like Mary does at the money in her wallet, and hope that measuring alone will bring about the needed change. Consider GardenJoy working harder and increasing productivity to improving results (the Y) without quantitatively examining which factors contribute to the success (the Xs of materials, supplies, level of quality, et cetera). Striving toward a goal without correct data - and in a disorganized and uncontrolled manner - most likely ends up in failure.

You can trace variation through data collection and statistics. If you then have insight into the variation, you can also identify where you need to improve the process to have as little variation as possible.

This then minimizes the number of defects in your process, and it increases profit, the quality of products, and employee satisfaction. Not all variation in the process falls within the upper and lower tolerance limits, and, therefore, there are defects. This means that there are variations in the process that are not acceptable to the customer and should not be present in the process. Let's say Julie buys a cellphone case for a 5.5-inch cellphone. Any variation with which your phone still fits in the case, for instance, 5.49 inch, will not be noticeable for the customer. However, we have a problem or defect if the phone no longer fits in the case; for example, if the case is 5-inch, the customer will not be satisfied. You can gain insight into this variation with the Six Sigma method. Based on these analyses, you can see how much variation is present, where this occurs most in the process and what causes it. That way, you also know where to adjust the process to minimize this variation.

But how do you know what is or is not acceptable to your customer? For this, you look at the Voice of the Customer (VOC): everything that falls within the limits of the Lower Specification Limit (LSL) and Upper Specification Limit (USL). On the other hand, you have the "Voice of the Process": the entire distribution (so also the part that falls outside the LSL and USL). The latter often expresses how the process works, but the VOC is most important because the customer comes first. With Six Sigma, we strive to have the entire process fall within the LSL and USL and, therefore, within the Voice of the Customer. The variation that is still present always falls within the quality limits of your customer. You've reached your goal when the variation present is entirely acceptable to your customer.

Chapter 8. Analyze: Finding Possible and Root Causes

After the Define and Measure Phases, we´ve now reached the Analyze Phase, great! But before we dive into the Analyze Phase, we need to take a step back, because we´re at a critical point of the process. We need to look back at what we´ve done, so we get rid of wrong data, bad assumptions, and incorrect goals. These errors will snowball in this phase, and we will analyze with the false data and spending a lot of time, effort, and money, making unnecessary improvements. Before analyzing the data, we check the previous phases. What is our problem, again, as we looked at in the first phase? Are we addressing the Voice of the Customer? Know that the more data you have, the more resources you'll need in the Analyze Phase. So, be sure that you're collecting data on the correct variables so that the right variables are analyzed if you're going to tackle a process project. For instance, when you're looking at something like your variances in your processes - as far as the quality that's being produced, for instance, defect rates. This is more of a *quantitative study* and needs professionals with high statistics and Six Sigma knowledge. Qualitative studies, such as any project regarding waste, need people with a Lean skillset. In the Analyze Phase, the project team will focus on analyzing the sources of variation that were found in the selected process. Based on the problem, the techniques to find more root causes will be selected. Afterward, the project team will analyze the value stream, i.e., the set of activities that create value for your customers. Finally, the project members will also focus on identifying process drivers. These are activities that have a significant influence on the outcomes of processes.

What is the Analyze Phase?

In the Measure phase, we obtained more information about the current status of the process and the nature and extent of the problem. In the Analyze phase, you assess the ongoing process and try to find the leading causes of the issues identified based on further analysis. In this phase, you'll analyze all the information and data that you've collected in the previous stage. You will need this information to be able to find out the cause of the defects, lousy quality, and waste. To reach reasonable conclusions, a significant challenge here is that your team sticks to this data and does not rely on its knowledge and experience. Based on the data, you can conclude what the root cause of the problem is. The principal activities we undertake in this phase are:

- Searching for specific patterns in the data
- Identifying where a lot of resources, such as time, energy, and money, are wasted

How this helps us:

- They prove we need to identify the root cause, identifying the root cause *instead of symptoms*
- You'll find ways to speed up the process without compromising quality
- Also, you identify critical variables in the process you need to control, as well as essential factors in the process that must be under control

All possible causes are first collected based on the process and statistical data. You first identify all possible influencing factors. By further analysis and application of statistical methods, you try to limit the extensive list of possible causes to a small number of root causes (also known as the Vital Few or Red Xs). Two types of analysis are needed to discover and validate the root causes. In the first place, you take a closer look at the data that was collected in the Measure Phase. This analysis is called data analysis. You also investigate the value flow for possible waste (process analysis). Performing data analysis is also called the "data door" and analyzing the value flow the "process door."

With the data analysis, you verify the possible root causes with the help of statistical techniques, think of the following:

- Applying tables, graphs, and key figures to summarize and present the data.
- Regression analysis to investigate the relationship of influence factors on the result.
- Performing hypothesis tests to show which root causes are statistically significant.

In process analysis, the emphasis is placed on investigating the *efficiency of the process.* You do this with instruments that can be used to analyze risks, identify wastage, and make a distinction between activities that add value and actions that don't. It's often more Lean-oriented techniques such as Ishikawa, FMEA, Value Stream Mapping (VSM), Process Mapping, and the Five Whys method. The most important analytical tool for process analysis is the VSM. With a VSM, you visualize the process on paper and then assess for process steps, whether they are value-adding or non-value-adding.

Data and process analysis are aimed at understanding the problem/process and finding the causes of process variability. The aim is to determine what the leading causes are and how they affect the problem. Here you look for the causal relationships between influencing factors (Xs) and the output (Y), and you substantiate this with facts. The associations found between input (X) and output (Y) not only explain why the current performance is as it is but also form the basis for searching for the solution (s) in the Improve phase. In other words: the root causes found to indicate the short, medium, and long-term opportunities for improving the process.

Value Stream Mapping: Identifying Waste Causes

Value Stream Mapping is a commonly used technique to gain insight into wastes within a process. Business processes are mapped with Value Stream Mapping (VSM). The order of the activities that bring about a product or service is analyzed.

A value is added to each activity. VSM aims to improve the business process continuously. The business process is shown schematically in a diagram. The process steps and the information and material flows are visually represented (present state). From the diagram, it becomes clear where there are possibilities for improvements. With this tool, employees gain a shared understanding of the current situation and more understanding of each other's work and problems. Also, Value Stream Mapping is a useful model for working towards an ideal situation (future state).

Before mapping out the current situation, the purpose of the analysis must first be determined, for example, reducing the lead time. The goals must be acceptable to employees. The customer value is then identified per product. Then a team is put together, involved in the activities in the value and information flow. Take these points of advice:

- First, make sure you identify the actions (process steps) and assign the correct order. Frameworks determine in which role the activity is performed.

- Second, ensure that the processing, waiting, and recovery time of activity is determined. The extent to which an activity is carried out correctly in one go is expressed as a percentage.
- Third, the efficiency of the process is calculated (processing time versus lead time).
- Fourth, we now have a better view of the process whereby we can identify wastes much better.

The purpose of using this tool is to map the current situation and to identify wastes. As we explained earlier in Lean, there are seven well-known wastes. Some experts also add an eighth waste: Talent. The other wastes are: Waiting, Over-processing, Inventory, Transport, Defects, and Motion.

After this, you can work according to a step-by-step plan:

- Determine in advance of which product, product family, or service the Value Stream is captured.
- Describe the current situation (Current State) in a step-by-step plan, including every step (including delays) required to deliver the product or service.
- Describe the desired step plan in the desired situation (Future State).
- Analyze the differences between the two schemes and determine the action points based on this and set priorities to make the required improvements.

The Five Whys Method

The *five whys method* is a simple but very effective Lean Six Sigma tool to identify the root cause of a problem. The technique was developed by Toyota to perform root cause analysis for production-related issues. It's one of the tools available for implementing a root cause analysis. Although it's simple in practice, the output can be advantageous. Applying the method is done by these steps:

- Identify the problem for which the root cause must be identified. Ask the question, *why did this problem arise?* The result is an answer with a new or different problem.
- Take the first answer (or problem) and ask the question again: *Why did this problem arise?*
- Repeat these steps at least five times. If you think you can continue, by all means, continue until you reach the root cause of the problem.

Once during a Lean Six Sigma training, an attendee came up with a solution to the problem from the get-go. The problem was: "The customer receives an order late from the supplier for the fifth time." The attendee said straight away: "Then they must follow a time management course or hire more people." When dealing with organizational problems, never think of solutions straight away, because you've no clue if this is even the root cause. Thus, we start applying the *five whys method*.

- The first question would be: "Why did the customer receive the order too late from the supplier?" Frequently, the answer can be a real surprise, such in this case.
  - The answer: "BlueTransport Inc., responsible for the delivery, did not have the correct address details of the customer."
- The second question would be: "Why doesn't BlueTransport Inc. have the correct customer address details?"
  - The answer: "The address on the shipment does not match the address of the customer?"
- The third question would be: "Why doesn't the shipping address match the customer's address?"
  - The answer: "The customer moved to a new city two months ago, and the new address is not yet included in the supplier's customer base."
- The fourth question would be: "Why is the customer's new address not yet included in the supplier's customer base?"

> o The answer: "The only CRM system administrator was ill for the past two weeks, and no one has thought of changing the address."
- The fifth question would be: "Why didn't anyone think about changing the address?"
  > o The answer and root cause: "No one knew how to make a change to the customer base using the CRM system."

In the end, the root cause had to do with the fact that no employee knew how to change an address using the CRM system. This is the reason why the company failed to deliver the order. Without continuously asking "why," we may never know that this was the pressing issue. Now that we know the "real" problem, i.e., the root cause, we can take the necessary steps to tackle it and fix it.

Hypothesis Testing

We use tests to prove relationships between one or more Xs and the Y. To test and show (in a meaningful way) whether the suspected link between X and Y exists, it's imperative to know what you're testing. In the Lean Six Sigma field, hypothesis testing is used to make a statement about the existence of a statistically significant relationship between cause (x) and effect (Y) or between two or more causes. But what is a hypothesis? In science, a hypothesis is a proposition that has not (yet) been proven and serves as the starting point of a theory, a statement, or a derivation. Therefore, we're talking about testing a hypothesis because we assume that there is one. A possible relationship exists between two or more variables or that one variable (x) influences the behavior (the outcome) of another variable (Y). However, the statement is not (yet) proven, because it needs testing. To be able to test a hypothesis adequately, we will have to define a proposition. A statement that indicates that there's a significant relationship or significant influence between variables. However, if we make a statement that such a connection or difference exists, then the inverse statement is also true, namely that this relationship or difference doesn't exist. Therefore, we always define two propositions with hypothesis testing, namely the so-called null hypothesis and the alternative.

- The Null Hypothesis (H0): there's no significant difference or relationship
- The Alternative hypothesis (Ha): there is a meaningful relationship or difference

Furthermore, there are a few critical elements for formulating a reasonable hypothesis, namely:

- **The team is suspecting a relationship between the variables.** Hypothesis testing is, of course, not arbitrarily, but based on suspicion of the existence of a particular relationship between variables.
- **They are statements, not questions.** It is crucial that a reasonable hypothesis is defined as a statement *and not as a question*. By drawing up a null hypothesis and an alternative hypothesis, we describe both possible outcomes, and it's up to the team to show which of the two is appropriate.
- **It can be tested/measured.** And last but not least, it is, of course, important that the hypothesis can be examined, which means that we must have measurement data by which we can say whether there is a relationship or difference or the absence thereof. Hypothesis testing makes sense when we are not examining the entire population, but have taken a sample from the people in our audience.

There are a few steps you can take to test hypotheses, whereby we go from a practical problem to a statistical problem, to statistical solutions, to practical solutions.

- First, define the research question. The research question is a direct consequence of the issue from the project charter. The Project Charter is a contract between client and

contractor: a communication document that the sponsor and project manager agree upon at the outset.
- Second, define the null hypothesis H0.
- Third, define the alternative hypothesis Ha.
- Fourth, determine the significance level.
- Fifth, collect measurement data and rate and test the data.
- Sixth, run a test with a statistical program like Minitab or SPSS and draw the statistical conclusion.
- Seventh, write down the conclusion in a practical way, so that all stakeholders can understand it.

Take, for instance, OnTheWay, an organization for traffic and tourism that's researching the ease of parking of two types of cars, namely electric cars and gasoline cars. This research is conducted - under the same circumstances - by 30 test subjects by having each person park both types of cars once. They defined the following research question: "Is the average parking time for both types of cars the same?" Afterward, they established hypotheses. H0: "There is no difference in the time required to park the cars," and Ha: The average difference to park both cars does exist." Then, they determine the significance level. Because this is a standard test whereby defects don't lead to severe consequences, a reliability level of 95% is acceptable. Then, OnTheWay collects the number of seconds it takes for the subjects to park the cars. Afterward, the rate and test the data by using a Paired t-test in the statistical program SPSS by IBM. Last - but not least - they write an informational and concise report of their findings in plain English. With this report, they can continue to the next phase, namely the improvement phase.

Let's take a look at what this phase is all about!

Chapter 9. Improve: Generating Solutions

Now that we have a good overview of Lean, Six Sigma, and Lean Six Sigma, it's time to focus on the practical side of Lean Six Sigma. In this chapter, we take a closer look at the Lean Six Sigma process and how you can implement the same. As explained previously in this book, there are two critical methodologies for implementing Lean Six Sigma in your organization, namely DMAIC and DMADV. In this chapter, you'll learn more about both these standard processes and their benefits, so that you can decide the process you'd like to follow.

What is the Improve Phase?

In the Improve phase, you conduct changes to the process so that the found defects, wastage, and extra costs - related to the needs of the customer and as identified in the Define Phase - are eliminated. This link with customer needs is essential. After all, you only work on the (root) causes that touch on the problem or need. These are the causes you identified in the previous phase, Analyze. In the Improvement Phase, you focus on the following:

> • You use tools and techniques to channel creative thinking and formulate adequate solutions to the related root causes.

You no longer blindly follow what management demands, but do your thinking based on the gathered data.

- Besides, you strive to learn as many best practices as possible. Many DMAIC projects have been conducted in all kinds of organizations. So, why not learn from others before trying things yourself? This will fast track your Lean Six Sigma projects.
- Also, in this phase, it's emphasized that you develop criteria with which you can select solutions. You determine the course to be followed that belongs to the chosen resolution and plan the full implementation thereof.

Always keep in mind that the objective of the Improve Phase is to *implement and verify the solution* to the problem. To determine the optimal setting for a process, specific techniques can be used, such as regression analysis or cost-benefit analysis. By adequately going through this phase, you don't get caught up in figuring solutions that don't apply to the found root cause or don't suit the available resources. Also, you'll develop more creative solutions that are related to the root cause and are proven in the past. With experience and gaining more knowledge of real case studies, you can substantiate why one solution is advised above another solution.

Steps Toward Improvement

In this phase, we'll identify, prioritize, and implement the improvements for the most critical inputs and outputs we discovered in the previous phase. The corresponding statistical formula is: $f(X1 + X2...) = Y$. The output we strive to attain is, of course, the fact that we've identified possible solutions and implemented the best to eliminate or, if not possible otherwise, reduce root causes as much as possible. Usually, we make an improvement plan to ensure proper implementation. Key questions surrounding the plan are: "What are we improving?" and "In what part of the process will we embed the solution?" After the plan, we move on to implementing a pilot. We never embed an improvement organization-wide from the get-go.

Instead, we figure out parts of a process where we can test the improvement. If the pilot is successful, slowly but surely, the improvement can be embedded into other parts of the process or other processes. Performing a pilot is crucial because it gives us crucial data to work with. If the pilot fails, we return to identifying improvements and test another one.

We can distill this phase in a couple of steps:

- First, make sure that the project team has reviewed all items that came about in the Analyze Phase. Check created documents, gathered data, and possible errors.
- Second, discuss with the team members an improved version of the business process you're tackling. This needs to be a process that would be wholly optimized for customer satisfaction.
- Third, it's advisable to make a transition plan. This will facilitate the move from the current process to the newly crafted process when doing so, take the PDCA (Plan, Do, Check, Act) cycle in mind.

Cost-Benefit Analysis

A cost-benefit analysis (CBA) is a systematic approach to estimate strong and weak points in, for instance, transactions, investments, business processes, or other activities. The predominantly monetary evaluation method is used to identify effective options and make responsible choices that both offer benefits and are cost-effective. However, in this process, values are also given to intangible issues such as the benefits associated with working in a specific area or possible loss of reputation after making risky strategic choices. The income and expenses are therefore expressed in terms of money and are adjusted for the time value of money. This is needed to use the net present value frequently. The cost-benefit analysis is used, among other things, for making purchase/production decisions, for example, in real estate investments, but also in decisions that affect society. In a social cost-benefit analysis, the external effects of a decision are also included in the evaluation. However, in most organizations, the focus is strictly on the cost benefits. There are various advantages this analysis brings to the table, such as the research into the viability of a project proposal, the evaluation of new purchases/investments, and the assessment of the desirability of a proposed policy.

These are the steps to make your cost-benefit analysis:

- **First of all, you need to determine the expected costs and benefits of the project.** Take the time to brainstorm about the costs associated with the project and compile a list of all possible costs. Do the same for all the benefits of the project result.
    - Some crucial questions that can be asked here are: Are there unexpected costs that may still be identified in advance? Are there advantages associated with the result that was not initially assumed?
    - Think of different forms of costs, like operating costs, personnel costs, real estate, facilities, and material costs. But also unnecessary costs such as time, energy, or a loss in customer satisfaction.
    - Types of benefits are higher revenue, more savings, better customer satisfaction, and more satisfied employees.
- **Second, express the costs and benefits in the same unit.** Where costs are relatively easy to communicate in terms of money, the benefits are slightly different. However, both costs and benefits must be expressed in the same unit since they must be compared. Therefore, think about the effects of the benefits that the project brings forth.
    - Related questions are: Is an increase in customer satisfaction to be expected? And will this provide extra revenue? A monetary value must be assigned to all these benefits.

- **Third, compare the costs and benefits.** In the final step, the value of the costs must be compared with the value of the benefits. To do this, calculate the total costs and the total benefits and compare these two values to determine whether the benefits outweigh the costs. Then make a decision based on the results of the comparison.

To further illustrate this take, BetterTextile Inc., an Eastern European manufacturer of textile. BetterTextile Inc. notices that earnings rose for the third consecutive year and has insufficient capacity to meet the rising demand for their textile in Western Europe. BetterTextile Inc. is considering tapping into a new market in Western Europe and requires more employees for this. The business premises must also be expanded, and the new employees will be provided with advanced tools and better training to hone their skills. Thus, BetterTextile Inc. made a cost-benefit analysis to determine whether the new strategy is worth pursuing. In this example, we assumed the following:

- BetterTextile Inc. expects to earn back the investment that they made after one year.
- The company expects productivity to increase by around 6% with better-trained staff using more advanced equipment.
- Also, BetterTextile Inc. expects revenue to increase by 30% after expanding capacity.
- Finally, BetterTextile Inc. hires additional staff for 200 hours per month for 40 dollars per hour.

When we take the benefits of $300,000 and costs of $210,500, we can say that BetterTextile Inc. will make a profit on this move. Of course, in real life, these assumptions have to be validated in more detail and with real data. But this will do for an illustration. The illustration shows that making such an analysis helps in making moves that may seem bold, but can turn out to be very profitable.

Solution Parameters and Generating Possible Solutions

A parameter is a letter in a formula that represents a constant. It's like the creator of the assignment doesn't want to reveal this continuous. Therefore, a parameter is something different than a variable. A variable is x or y: a letter that assumes all kinds of possible values, and for each of those values, you get a point on the graph. You can plot a variable on the x-axis or the y-axis. A parameter has only one constant value, *but we don't know it yet*. What are the consequences of the graph? If you have a function regulation with a parameter in it, then you have a problem because you can't draw points (x, y), you cannot enter a formula in your graphing calculator. The only thing you can do is replace the parameter with a number you want, like parameter = 1. Then you have a formula without a parameter, and you can draw it. Then choose another number, parameter = 2, and draw the graph again. You can continue for a while, and then you get a collection of a lot of graphs. This is called a chart bundle. A function description with a parameter, therefore, never includes one graph, but always a graphing bundle.

In Lean Six Sigma, we see something similar. In the Improve Phase, we tend to make use of so-called solution parameters. These solution parameters help us select the right improvements to solve an issue. The first step in doing so is by developing a *decision statement*. Utilizing brainstorming, we can gather various solutions to clarify the purpose of the decision the team is going to make. While forming your decision statement, think of matters like how you'll manage customer expectations and how you'll react and evaluate to possible decisions the team took in the past. For the second step, you need to formulate a list of around ten criteria to help you solve the issue at hand. With criteria, we can look at the list of possible improvements we've generated and tested them against the criteria. The criteria can be divided into two forms, namely the "Musts" and the "Wants." For the last step, refine the solution criteria as much as possible before you use them to select the right solutions or generate other solutions. New solutions could be made, for instance, by combining two solutions or improvements you found. All team members should be aware of the implications of the criteria; there should be no room for ambiguity.

It's not always easy to figure out innovative ideas; humans often need a little push to wake up our creative sides. The SCAMPER technique is a useful brainstorming technique to help us do just that. With this method, one can produce ideas for new products and services by asking various questions. The questions generate creative ideas for developing new products and improving current products.

- First, select an existing product or service.
- Second, asks questions by using the SCAMPER method. It's most useful to do this with the team.
- Third, categorize the answers into something like "useful," "maybe useful," and "not useful." Or, you can use something like the Likert scale to generate the best solutions.

SCAMPER is an acronym for Substitute, Combine, Adapt, Magnify/Modify, Purpose, Minify/Eliminate, Rearrange/Reverse. These are questions you can ask for each element:

- Substitute:
  o Are there materials or resources that we can substitute to improve the product?
  o Can we use the product/service for other purposes?
- Combine:
  o What will happen if the product/service is combined with another product?
  o Could the product/service be used for a different purpose?
- Adapt:
  o What other context would the product/service fit in?

- - How can the product/service be adjusted so that it runs better?
- Magnify/Modify:
  - How can we adequately modify the shape or appearance of the product/service?
  - What can be added to the product/service to make it better?
- Purpose:
  - Are there other people than our current customers that will benefit from this product/service?
  - Can the waste from this product/service be reused?
- Eliminate/Minify:
  - What would this product/service look like if it was simplified?
  - Which functions or components can be omitted?
- Rearrange/Reverse:
  - What happens if parts of the product/service are assembled in a different order?
  - What happens if the product is turned over?

Chapter 10. Control: Sustaining Improvement

After the Improvement Phase, it's finally time for the last phase of the DMAIC cycle, namely the Control Phase. The purpose of the Control phase is to help attain the desired results in the organization. Although the problem may already be resolved, the team must not forget to take this phase seriously and prevent the problem from reoccurring. The best way to achieve this is to guarantee improvement with "Poka Yoke" solutions, which are not dependent on the employee. This is not always possible, and then the solution still depends on the employee's working method. This is particularly the case if the solution results in a different method. Possibilities for guaranteeing an improvement, in this case, are the drafting of new work instructions, the provision of training, and the adaptation of quality documents such as the Control Plan. In the Control phase, the team also figures out how much resources were saved, and this is compared with the expected savings at the start of the project. Afterward, the order is formally returned to the client, the Champion. After all, the job of the Champion or the department manager is to value the team for the performance delivered.

What is the Control Phase?

In the control phase, the goal is to anchor the implemented changes and ensure that the issues don't return. To achieve this, you monitor the most critical x's and y's with the help of a control chart. Another tool that is often used in the control phase is a Control Plan. These techniques and tools all help with the essential checking we need to do. Why do we even bother checking? Well, because we want to be sure that the progress we made is lasting. Your employees need procedures and tools to support changes in the way they perform their work. The team must pass on what they have learned to the process owner, and they must be sure that all parties involved in the process are properly trained to handle the new procedures. Therefore, a few key activities take place in this phase:

- First, we ensure that new or improved procedures are documented adequately.
- Second, we make sure that every related employee gets the necessary training to work with the new procedures.
- Third, we set up procedures to detect signals of things going wrong in the process, for instance.
- Fourth, the daily management of the new/improved process is delegated to the process owner, who will then oversee if the process works as planned.

If the team did a good job, this would result in many benefits. It will prevent relapse because changing people's habits means more than just turning on a switch. The above action points should make it easier for employees to get used to new procedures and not fall back in their old habits. Furthermore, it helps you respond swiftly to future problems. If you follow essential signals in the process carefully, you will be able to react quickly if new issues arise. The faster you respond, the higher the chance that you will discover the root cause and find a solution. Finally, it creates a culture whereby we are continuously learning and improving. There is a chance that other people in your organization will do the same or similar work you've done. If you document the work you've done, the obstacles you faced, and how you overcame them, others in similar roles can learn from this.

The Control Plan

Being in control is essential when changing or improving a business process. It's no coincidence that the final phase of the DMAIC cycle is the Control Phase. You want to go through this phase to guarantee that the new working method is followed so that you do not fall back (consciously or unconsciously) in the old way of doing things. In practice, frequently, we see this relapse happen as soon as there is pressure or stress. The old way of working is familiar, and the outcome is known. It's precisely in these situations that it's essential to monitor the process to prevent colleagues from falling into old behavior or bad habits. All operational elements that we want to watch and control come together within Lean Six Sigma in the Control Plan, also known as the assurance plan. For each component, we indicate which concrete indicators we want to monitor, how we are going to do this, and what we do if the indicator goes beyond the set limits.

So, how do we make a control plan? To make one, take a look at these points and the related example:

- **Describe the parts (Y) of a process you would like to control.** Take InnoSub, a technology advisory firm that helps small businesses gain subsidies for working on innovative technologies that serve society. For this first step, the subsidy application process of the firm has been adjusted so that the time from "request" to "pending request" is within one week.
- **Then, determine the measurable indicators (Xs) of this selected component.** For InnoSub, there are a couple of quantifiable indicators. Think of processing time of checking subsidy documents, amount of available employees, number of cases in the queue. You work out steps 3-5 per indicator;

for this illustration, we take the "number of cases in the queue."

• **Now, you can prepare your measurement plan that includes how you'll measure the performance of the process and who will do the measuring.** InnoSub's Subsidy manager measures the "number of cases in queue" twice a week, on Monday and Friday at 10 pm.

• **Set related boundaries: when should action be taken?** The Lean Six Sigma team who worked on improving this process concluded that action must be taken if there are more than 15 files in the queue and no employees available to take these on.

• **Determine what you do if the indicators exceed the limits employing an OCAP (Out of Control Plan).** When things go wrong, InnoSub figured out a counteraction: call in the help of a few remote contractors to help deal with the remaining files and bring it down to at least 15. It's better to get the number back to zero as much as possible, but it cannot exceed the 15.

Control Chart

The control chart is the heart of "Statistical Process Control": Keeping a process under statistical control. The control chart is a graph that shows trends, shifts, or patterns in the output of a process over time. The purpose of the control chart is to discover whether the process is stable and under control. Take GreenLeaves, a company based in London that produces tea bags. Let's say the weight is measured for numerous tea bags; this weight can then be plotted in the chart. Essential to the control chart is the average ("centerline") and the so-called control limits we discussed in a previous chapter, namely the upper control limit (UCL) and lower control limit (LCL). These are the limits that indicate how much the process may deviate from the average. For this example, let's take a UCL of 2,5, an LCL of 1,4, and an average of 1,7 grams. The distance between the control limits indicates how much variation in the process can be expected. Observations that fall outside this space are "outliers," these are matters that demand further investigation. For instance, if GreenLeaves were to make tea bags of 3 grams, these would be outliers, because it's above the UCL of 2,5 grams.

Earlier, we addressed normal variation and the unexpected, unique variation. The latter is a variation that occasionally occurs and can break the process you're controlling. This is due to the influence of a demonstrable cause. For the tea bags that weigh too much, there is probably an unusual variation. Something in the process has ensured that these tea bags are too heavy. When we've figured out there are outliers in the process we're attempting to control, we can find the root causes of these with various Lean Six Sigma tools, like the Five Whys method we already addressed or the Ishikawa diagram. Besides, it's fundamental to look for patterns in the data. These patterns can help you be in "real control" of situations like these popping up. The ideal situation is that you intervene at the right moment and can foresee an outlier from rising to the surface.

The control chart is an example of a tool that can be used in more than one phase. It can be used in both the Analyze Phase and Control Phase. In the former, it's used to investigate whether the process to be improved is stable, and in the latter, it's used to recognize when a process shows signs of losing control. It's a great tool because it says a ton about the process you're controlling. However, the main disadvantage is that it doesn't say anything about whether the process meets the needs and/or desires of your customers. Why? Because the control limits (UCL and LCL) are often attained by using statistics and aren't the measures used by the customer.

Now imagine that the customer of Greanleaves wants smaller tea bags, with a minimum weight of 0,7 grams and a maximum weight of 1,2 grams. Our process will not be able to meet the wishes of the customer since our tea bags vary between 2,5 and 1,4 grams. As I mentioned multiple times throughout this book, Lean Six Sigma projects are all about striving for processes that meet the needs and desires of customers. Without a control chart, you're left in the dark regarding the organization's current process performance. By figuring out a way to deal with the inevitable variation and then improving processes by listening to the customer, we create a robust process that puts a smile on the customer's face.

Mistake Proofing: Poka Yoke

Poka Yoke is a Japanese term that means "error prevention" and was developed by an engineer at Toyota in the 1960s. Poka Yoke is used to prevent and resolve defects in the production process so that quality control afterward is no longer necessary (or to a far less degree). In Lean Manufacturing and Six Sigma, in particular, Poka Yoke is one of the most common methods for making sure that production runs smoothly from start to finish. What does Poka Yoke mean? "Poke" means "unintended error," while "yoke" means "to avoid" or "occurrence" in Japanese. By using Poka Yoke, mistakes are pretty much impossible to make, and the result is the right action being forced, ensuring there are no misunderstandings. It's all about using measures that stop mistakes from happening.

Poka Yoke includes many simple solutions that are also useful and cheap, and they are easily integrated into your design or one of the intermediate steps. Perhaps one of the best examples is a mobile phone SIM card. It can only go into the phone in one way, and that means there is no room for error. Poka Yoke is one of the most powerful tools, warning you of errors and allowing for quick reactions to stop deviations. It fits perfectly with Lean Six Sigma and, as such, is worth a look in terms of the DMAIC phases:

- **Define** – this phase involves describing and defining the problem that is causing the error or defect. The description is objective - with no direct conclusions. In the production process, the workplace can be observed, also called "Gemba," the Japanese word meaning "actual place." In your context, that could mean the factory, the manufacturing plant, and so on. The process runs in the workplace, and there is every chance that what is causing the problem is hidden. If the user is causing the problem, that problem should be defined objectively from the user's point of view.

- **Measure** – This phase tends to be applied to the more complex issues in production. Tests determine how much this problem happens, and that is then converted to a percentage. The higher it is, the more important it becomes to tackle the problem and solve it where it is caused. As well as production errors, user errors can also happen. In this case, test-groups are deployed for testing the product for a set length of time. The outcome is used to solve the problem.
- **Analysis** – this phase shows if you can apply a Poka Yoke measure. The process goes through a thorough analysis to trace where the defect is, and it is only then that a solution can be devised.
- **Improve** – the analysis provides the information needed to tackle the problem, devise the solution, and implement it. Many times, a Poka Yoke solution may be applied to great effect, ensuring that the mistake will not be made again.
- **Control** – in the final phase, the adjustments are looked at, and the effects measured. If you use a Poka Yoke measure and it works well, eliminating the risks of other potential errors, you get the "Zero Quality Control," meaning the requirement or personal inspection is removed because the potential of human error is removed.

There are two different Poka Yoke solutions for solving production problems:

- **Visual Aids/Steering Mean** – these are visible, showing the method clearly. Think of a warning traffic sign or a pictogram. The steering revolves around behavior and deviation warnings. Going back to that warning traffic sign, it may light red when a driver is going too fast or go green when the driver is going at the correct speed.

- **Compulsory Means/Fail-Safe (SF)** – with this one, users are forced into doing or not doing something. Let's say a highway has been closed for maintenance; message signs are used to force drivers down from three to two lanes of traffic, and red crosses are used to indicate the closed lane.

To further illustrate this, take the following example from HelloWeather, a company focused on making eco-friendly rain gear. Customers have complained that after a couple of weeks of use, cracks appear at the bottom of their newest Hello Raincoat. HelloWeather follows these steps to fix the problem the Poka Yoke way:

- **Define.** We start by objectively defining the problem. When putting on and taking off the Hello Raincoat a couple of times, cracks appear. The definition can be used to see how the suit is put on and taken off and in which order; first, insert the right arm and then the left arm (or vice versa), pull the zipper from bottom to top, pull the hood over the head, etc. Taking the coat off is in the reverse order.
- **Measure.** A test group can put on and take off the Hello Raincoat a few times a day, for several days. It can then be shown in samples how many of the test subjects had a coat that had cracks after the test period.
- **Analysis.** To know where the error is, it is wise to see what exactly happens when the coat is put on and off by the test group. The problem seems to be with the zipper. The light polyamide material that the coat is made of is not flexible enough when the coat is put on or taken off. As a result, there is pressure on the zipper, especially on the lower part, which quickly creates cracks/holes at this location.
- **Improve.** Now that we know how the holes appear at the bottom of the zipper, we can look at adjustments. The zipper is traditionally placed vertically in the suit. The solution is more straightforward than expected. By sewing the zipper diagonally in the suit, there is less pressure on the underside

of the zipper when getting in and out. This reduces the chance of cracks/holes.

• **Check.** The suit can be taken directly into production and offered for sale. To be fully assured that this is the solution for the cracks/holes at the bottom of the zipper, a test group can again be used, exactly as we did in the Measure Phase. With Poka Yoke, it's not directly about the test and measurement results, but the *real solution that is found.*

Chapter 11. Lean Six Sigma with Agile and Scrum

Since the time of Henry Ford, manufacturers were keen to realize more effective and efficient processes. With the rise of various car manufacturers, such as Toyota, new methods were developed to squeeze as much productivity in processes as possible. In the past, organizations assumed they worked efficiently and effectively enough. The opposite was the truth. They used to work with something we now see as obscure and highly ineffective and inefficient, namely the waterfall method. To tackle projects, they focused on various phases, namely first gathering requirements, performing analysis, designing the product, creating/coding it, testing it, and operating it. The major flaw in this system is that each phase in this method is completed in a vacuum! This means that professionals of all stages don't communicate with each other, and an organization only moves forth when a phase is completed (which is never the case in the dynamic world we live in!).

There was room for lots of improvement, and luckily this improvement came about when Hirotaka Takeuchi wrote a paper wherein he addressed the crux of what we would now call an *agile methodology*. It didn't take long before more agile methodologies popped up in different branches, such as Extreme Programming (XP), Kanban, and Scrum. It was only in the year 2001 within software development that a group of professionals came together to write the "Agile Manifesto." They included the basic principles of Agile working extracted from the various agile methodologies that were already practiced. Agile is now spreading rapidly to all types and parts of organizations. There are already hundreds of thousands of Agile practitioners around the world, and this number is only increasing. Especially Scrum has made a tremendous rise in organizations of different sizes, in various industries, in different countries all around the world. Let's take a closer look.

Agile breaks up significant product developments, in short, well-arranged periods (iterations) of two to a maximum of four weeks. Those iterations are small stand-alone projects that are managed by Timeboxing. The Agile approach enables a project team to quickly adapt the project to a changed situation or desires of the customer. Agile is the approach that is suitable for the dynamic world we live in. This is in contrast to a traditional project approach, in which a team tries to avoid change as much as possible by, on the one hand, laying down the specifications in detail and, on the other hand, setting up a formal process. People who flourish in an Agile team are people who are not afraid of change and are less inclined to look for certainties. Being able to start something without having a well-known result is very important. Agile is not only suitable for relatively simple business projects. Agile can be a perfect companion for complex and long-term projects too. Agile splits complex projects with iterations or sprints, making them more manageable. If objectives or circumstances change during the project, this is anything but a problem within Agile. It's essential here that the organization in question is one with an open, communicative culture. Scrum is easy to apply, and there is hardly any overhead. A Scrum team is self-managing and involves every team member in a project, including the customer, the user, and the client. Fast, clear insights, and clear expectations for all parties, deliver the desired product at the right time.

Agile and Lean Six Sigma are two philosophies with similar ideas. Agile is short and cyclical, which means that it is possible to anticipate market demand and customer wishes faster and better. Also, Agile contains the tools to repair a defect if it occurs quickly. This is because a 2-4 week cycle (the sprints/iterations) is used instead of a monthly or annual cycle. The idea of a Lean Startup outlined by author and entrepreneur Eric Ries also fits well with Agile thinking. In the book The Lean Startup, for example, the Minimum Viable Product (MVP) is mentioned. This (part of a) product already works and meets specific minimum requirements, but is not yet perfect or complete. This method can enormously shorten the "Time to Market." This is because the customer immediately receives certain functionality to get started. An additional advantage: feedback from users returns faster and contributes to the further development of the product.

Just like Lean Six Sigma, Agile pays a lot of attention to (customer) value and errors. A critical Lean Six Sigma principle is: "never pass a defect!" For example, FMEA (Failure Mode and Effect Analysis) is a technique that assesses the risks and effects of failure within the Lean philosophy and formulates countermeasures. Also, "Poka Yoke" - think of the SIM card that can only enter your phone in one way - is an important principle to prevent errors from the design itself. In the beginning, Agile projects focus a lot on business value. In Lean Six Sigma terms, this is called the "Voice of the Business (VOB)." Besides, applying FMEA makes it immediately clear what the customer finds essential, within Lean Six Sigma, the "Voice of the Customer (VoC)," but also whether the objectives are achievable within the set time. Besides, Agile is also focused on visualizing the progress of the "User Stories," such as requirements from customers. All ties could even tie in with another Agile methodology, such as Kanban. The Kanban methodology makes visualization possible, a technique that is also frequently used within Lean Six Sigma.

It sometimes seems that Agile, Lean Six Sigma, and Scrum are entirely different methods and that you should opt for a specific technique. The opposite is exact: the techniques overlap and complement each other. The trick is to get the items that work best for your organization from the different approaches. But how do you know which parts you could best use in your organization? It is, therefore, necessary, *before you start,* to exchange ideas with a consultant or professional in your organization.

Lean Six Sigma is usually used in standardized environments, such as production processes. Scrum is widely used for creative and innovative projects, no matter what industry. But with this separate approach, you exclude projects and processes that can benefit from a combined approach. In a production environment, for example, you can let the development and production of a product go hand in hand by combining Lean Six Sigma and Scrum, for example, in the form of Extreme Manufacturing. A good example is the Toyota Prius. Toyota, the birthplace of Lean, has used Scrum to develop its innovative hybrid car. The Prius was delivered within 15 months, from idea to working car. How have Lean Six Sigma and Scrum strengthened each other here? Lean elements came back in placing customer demand first and learning from mistakes. In Lean environments, the discovery of a fault means that you halt the production process and immediately resolve it as a team. At the same time, the Scrum approach helped in dealing with the uncertainties in the development process, which they were able to navigate thanks to the sprints.

Scrum provides practical tips for Lean Six Sigma principles. Scrum creates, among other things, flow and pull through multidisciplinary teams, quick deliveries, and the incorporation of interim feedback. Thanks to the sprints, you can continuously check whether you are still delivering value for the customer. Take this practical illustration of both methodologies:

- Lean Six Sigma principle #1: Specify a value for the customer.
    - Scrum approach: This principle ties in nicely with the fact that the Product Owner (one of the most

critical roles in Scrum), has the important task of continuously translate the customer wishes to a backlog with related tasks to fulfill these wishes. These tasks are then prioritized, tackling the most valuable items first.
- Lean Six Sigma principle #2: Identify the value stream.
   - Scrum approach: The complete value stream is combined in one Scrum project team. As a result, the waiting time is drastically shortened, and it's possible to respond to pending work with more flexibility.
- Lean Six Sigma principle #3: Create more flow in processes.
   - Scrum approach: Through intensive cooperation in small teams that work with short iterations, fast delivery, and feedback moments, waste such as transfer, waiting, errors, inventory, and overproduction are prevented.
- Lean Six Sigma principle #4: Create more pull.
   - Scrum approach: Working in sprints of approximately 1-3 weeks ensures rapid delivery and flexibility. You can respond directly to dynamic customer demand.
- Lean Six Sigma principle #5: Strive for perfection.
   - You get perfection through continuous learning and improvement. After every sprint, there is a review in which the product or service and work process are evaluated. The purpose of this is to make the process run even better in the next sprint.

All in all, it's precisely the combination of Lean Six Sigma and Agile methodologies, such as Scrum, that provides dynamicity and flexibility for your organization. I would, therefore, advise you to reinforce one approach with another whenever you can.

Chapter 12. Mistakes to Avoid in Lean Six Sigma

Anything worthwhile takes time. And anything worthwhile takes failures. Although failure is inevitable to run adequate Lean Six Sigma projects, it can also be very beneficial. It can reveal where there's room for improvement, give us ideas for what to try next, exposes our weaknesses, and grants us opportunities we wouldn't have thought about. No doubt, having clear goals and entering Lean Six Sigma projects with a positive mindset is vital to achieving success. Although failures may be inevitable, it doesn't stop us from learning from them and learning from other people's faults. This can help us not to make the same mistakes again or not make the in the first place.

First, avoid analysis paralysis. During the analysis phase, you may tend to keep going and going with, for instance, the root cause analysis so that you lose sight of the most crucial reason for the improvement project, namely, the critical reason for making a difference and seeing the positive opportunities for your company. It's vital to limit the scope of the project and to prevent you from taking all side roads available to you. Save these options for future projects, but keep the original scope. I know it can be challenging to determine when you should stop analyzing and start improving. But try to see this decision as an impartial decision and weigh the pros and cons. You are ready to move to the next phase if you can ensure that you know enough about the process, the problem, and founded root causes to come up with useful, innovative solutions. The project champion, the project supervisor, has an important role. He/she must keep an eye on company interests when answering these questions and keep the team on the right track.

Second, don't get overwhelmed. Achieving Six Sigma (3.4 defects per 1 million options) can be a beautiful end goal, but with one project, you're not likely to achieve anything near this precision. In Lean Six Sigma projects, the usual trend we see is to go from two sigma to three sigma and then to four sigma. Small, bite-sized projects ensure that your performance is moving in the right direction, so be prepared to accept a small increase in the sigma value of the processes, but always remember that these modest increases, day in, day out, will help you win in the long term.

Third, don't *just* conclude! Many managers tend just to draw conclusions when they face a problem. Sudden decisions can be costly and be an obstacle in addressing the cause of the problem. Doing something randomly, or just calling something randomly in business, without collecting and analyzing facts and data is not the best approach to solve complex business problems. Lean Six Sigma involves understanding what the problem is and then going through some steps to understand it better (define, measure); dig deeper to found the root cause (analyze); look at the different solutions and then choose the best (improve) and implement this solution and retain its benefits (control). Although this approach sounds very simple and meaningful, it feels unnatural to many executives who think they know everything best. Look at the enormous amount of decisions that are taken every year about production systems, warehouses, office spaces, IT systems, company reorganizations, new products, organization training programs, and more. These decisions are often random "solutions" that popped up during an executive meeting. But companies often find out half a year or a year later that these "solutions" do not meet the needs of the customer.

Fourth, thinking, "we know it all already." A brief look at books about Lean Six Sigma or a quick look at your processes can make you feel that your organization "does it already." Many managers think that their problems will solve themselves if they use a systematic problem-solving process. But often they don't think about solution options before they implement them. Or they do not sufficiently test the different options. You may think, "We are already using flowcharts or root cause analysis methods." Many organizations use these techniques, but often without first understanding the real requirements of the process from the customer's perspective. If you do not implement Lean Six Sigma in a structured way, you will never fully use the power of process analysis techniques to find out how existing processes work. Real support from management for such a process also analyzes rare but very much needed. This creates a bottleneck in many Lean Six Sigma projects: the employees want to change with Lean Six Sigma, but the management wants to do "it" how it was always doing "it," whatever that's supposed to mean. A well-designed Lean Six Sigma program is based on existing knowledge, places improvements in a framework in which everyone is involved, and introduces a comprehensive set of tools for the entire organization.

Fifth

, embracing false beliefs about Lean Six Sigma. If you want Lean Six Sigma to work in practice, you will have to eradicate some false notions, namely:

- **Thinking that Lean Six Sigma is only helpful when an organization wants to improve production processes.** The methodology is not necessarily exclusively related to production processes, and this is proven by various companies that deliver other services than manufactured products, such as Software as a Service.
- **Knowing that Lean Six Sigma is everything we need.** As we mentioned above, doing things in a vacuum is never the right decision. The same goes for Lean Six Sigma, and this

approach works best with other methodologies, such as Scrum. Take the best from these worlds to get the projects off the ground.

- **Thinking that Lean Six Sigma is nothing but statistics.** Without question, statistical tools and measurements are essential in this methodology, but it's not the end! There are many other external and internal aspects to it, such as putting the customers first, but also stimulating the necessary cultural changes within the organization or department.

Conclusion

In this book, we took a look at the most important elements of the famous Lean Six Sigma methodology. In this book, we took a look at two parts. The first being The Essentials and the second being The Process. These phases were filled with various practical chapters to get yourself familiarized with the essential concepts to run Lean Six Sigma projects. The first part, The Essentials, was covered in Chapters 1-4. You learned more about how Lean came about at Toyota, and you learned it's principles and concepts. Some of its powerful principles are: Specify Value, Identify the Value Stream, Create Flow, Pull, and Pursue Perfection. These principles help in eliminating all forms of wastes, namely: Transport, Inventory, Movement, Waiting, Overproduction, Overprocessing, and Defects.

Also, we delved more in-depth in the various roles present in the Lean Six Sigma approach. The multiple roles are related to different colored belts to indicate responsibility levels and tasks. The roles I addressed were: the leadership team, sponsor, implementation leader or champion, the coach, and team member, and process owner. The belts discussed were: The Yellow Belt, Orange Belt, Green Belt, Black Belt, and Master Black Belt Afterward, we took a look at the methodology, countless benefits, and possible training and certifications you can get.

Implementing Lean Six Sigma comes with numerous benefits. Lean Six Sigma includes the integration of the speed of Lean and the quality of Six Sigma. Six Sigma improves quality (error reduction) by better understanding the business process and ensures a balanced infrastructure. Lean stands for speed by eliminating steps in processes. Both are needed to reduce the costs of complexity in business processes. An essential aspect of Lean Six Sigma is process improvement. According to the underlying philosophy, a group of professionals is needed to effectively and efficiently solve problems.

Above all, a team of professionals, trained in aspects of Lean Six Sigma, works on a problem that is relevant to the organization and its customers. Lean Six Sigma strives for higher quality in less time. To achieve that objective, the organization and process flows of a company must be clear, and everything that is unacceptable to the customer must be eliminated. The people working in different processes can deliver more in a team and share expertise and ideas to solve a problem. All decisions are based on data and facts.

Lean Six Sigma can help a manager achieve goals such as cost savings, more efficient use of the budget, and better customer satisfaction in a structured and substantiated manner. Lean principles are applied to get speed in the processes. As a result of this, it's necessary to recognize waste. Statistics also adds something to process improvement. Is there a visible trend in a process, or is it just coincidence? The following applies to Lean Six Sigma: we intervene only when it's necessary because intervention often costs extra time, energy, and money and can harm the morale of the team. It must also be possible to quantify relationships, for example, between lead times and the number of ongoing projects. To improve, the process must first be understood. By using the DMAIC cycle, we can do the same.

In the second part of this book, The Process, we took a more detailed look at the most critical process surrounding Lean Six Sigma, namely the DMAIC cycle. We took a look at every phase in the cycle and essential tools and techniques. For the Define Phase, we took a look at the Voice of the Customer and Process Mapping with the SIPOC technique. For the Measure Phase, we learned more about data and defects. Furthermore, we learned about finding root causes by using techniques such as the Five Whys method in the Analyze Phase. When the Analyze Phase was cleared, the Improve Phase helped us generate solutions to tackle the root causes we found. Finally, with techniques such as Poka Yoke, it's possible to keep control of the process after the issue was fixed. Furthermore, we learned that applying Lean Six Sigma doesn't happen in a vacuum. Instead, it happens by being much involved with your customers and team members. These are precisely the elements that are present in agile methodologies, such as Scrum. Thus, it's possible to incorporate various aspects of the Scrum approach with Lean Six Sigma.

There are also mistakes you can better avoid for any worthwhile success. When you avoid analysis paralysis, don't get overwhelmed, don't just draw conclusions, don't think that you "know it already," and stop embracing false beliefs regarding Lean Six Sigma, you're well on your way to creating, keeping, and delivering more valuable projects as a project manager!

Check out another book by Robert McCarthy

Resources

https://www.pmi.org/about/learn-about-pmi/what-is-project-management

https://zenkit.com/en/blog/7-popular-project-management-methodologies-and-what-theyre-best-suited-for/

https://activecollab.com/blog/project-management/project-manager-roles-and-responsibilities

https://www.smartsheet.com/content-center/best-practices/project-management/project-management-guide/how-choose-project-management-methodology

https://www.wrike.com/project-management-guide/faq/what-is-lean-project-management/

https://www.goskills.com/Lean-Six-Sigma

https://www.pmi.org/learning/library/lean-project-management-7364

https://www.projectengineer.net/how-to-perform-lean-project-management/

https://barryoreilly.com/what-is-lean-enterprise-and-why-it-matters/

https://www.whatislean.org/lean-enterprise/

https://leanstartup.co/build-dream-lean-team/

https://www.manufacturing.net/home/article/13193627/what-is-a-lean-team

https://www.revelx.co/blog/what-is-lean-analytics/

https://www.mendix.com/agile-framework/

https://www.softwareadvice.com/resources/agile-frameworks/

https://www.productplan.com/glossary/agile-framework/

https://blog.orangescrum.com/2018/11/step-by-step-guide-to-agile-project-management.html

https://www.cmswire.com/information-management/agile-vs-scrum-vs-kanban-weighing-the-differences/

https://blog.forecast.it/implementation-of-scrum-7-steps

https://hygger.io/blog/5-steps-of-kanban-implementation/

Printed in Great Britain
by Amazon